Crosscurrents/MODERN CRITIQUES

Crosscurrents/MODERN CRITIQUES

Harry T. Moore, *General Editor*

Nineteenth-Century French Romantic Poets

Robert T. Denommé

WITH A PREFACE BY
Harry T. Moore

SOUTHERN ILLINOIS UNIVERSITY PRESS
Carbondale and Edwardsville

FEFFER & SIMONS, INC.
London and Amsterdam

For My Students
Past, Present and To Come

Preface

In this book Robert T. Denommé has given us an expert account of French Romanticism and a valuable exposition of its leading poets. All this is within the range of university studies, and in that area the volume should prove helpful indeed in providing students with important clues and conclusions. But Professor Denommé has done something more: he has written a book which the general reader, who in English-speaking countries knows little of French Romanticism, will find interesting and informative.

The forty-page opening chapter, "Toward a Definition of Romanticism," supplies a historical background for the exploration of the individual poets. Most of the writers of the preceding period, the Enlightenment, had "felt that too great an insistence upon the function of the imagination in the cognitive process could impair man's rational powers to the extent of reducing his ability to act with common sense." As Professor Denommé further points out, these philosophes of the eighteenth century shared Plato's conception of the poet as a dangerous wild man. But François-René de Chateaubriand, one of the Romantic pioneers, believed with many of his contemporaries "that the single-dimensional inheritance of the Enlightenment was incapable of piercing through the essential truths of the universe." Many of these early Romantics were frustrated, however, by the policies of Napoleon I, who attempted to keep literature rigidly "classical" and who exiled Madame de Staël, "the first significant theorist of French Romanticism."

Professor Denommé deals with such events of the time and also gives a fine analysis of the conflict of ideas from which Romanticism emerged, belatedly but triumphantly, with the success of Victor Hugo's play, Hernani. That was in 1830; the conservatives were against this drama when it was put on at the Comédie-Française, but Hugo's young supporters outshouted, outclapped, and outstamped the traditionalists.

Hugo, the most important Romanticist, receives fuller treatment in this book than the other poets considered: Alphonse de Lamartine, Alfred de Vigny, and Alfred de Musset. I have the impression that these men are not well known here in America except among those who have specialized in French; even Hugo, the true world figure among these Romantic poets, is neglected over here except for his novel, Les Misérables. But the present volume should help to make these writers better known; one of its features is the translation of every poem quoted from his work and those of the other writers examined here. And very good translations these are, too—accurate and, in spite of the prose form, carrying over much of the vividness of the originals.

In his essays, the author sticks almost entirely to the poems themselves, their meaning and their general significance in the Romantic movement. He draws only occasionally upon biography, as for example when he explains the appearance of occult ideas in Hugo's poems after he became interested in spiritualism following the death of his daughter. But such excursions beyond the texts occur rarely. For the most part Professor Denommé provides readings of the poems, readings which will interest the experts and which should attract many general readers to this new consideration of the early poets of the French Romantic movement.

HARRY T. MOORE

Southern Illinois University
August 16, 1968

Contents

Introduction

The following chapters are a study of the theory and practice of poetry by the leading exponents of French Romanticism. A conscious attempt has been made to set the aesthetic, social, and philosophical implications found in the major poems within the historical framework from which they emerged. The term poetry is considered in its broadest sense; the epic, satirical, and didactic expression of the poets in question are studied and juxtaposed to their more obvious lyrical verse. The first chapter, "Toward a Definition of Romanticism," is largely theoretical in nature in its effort to incorporate the ideas and trends of the French and Continental writers whose work bears a direct relevance to the development of nineteenth-century French Romantic poetry. The subsequent chapters on Lamartine, Vigny, Hugo, and Musset serve as illustrations of the theories discussed in the first essay.

To make this study available to the general reader as well as to students in French and Comparative literatures, I have translated into English the passages that are quoted to illustrate the points that are made. Likewise, I have given prose approximations of all the verse that is cited; no attempt has been made to translate such verse in poetical form. My intention has been primarily to capture the mood and sense of the poetic fragments that have been quoted. The original French forms have been preserved in the text to meet the requirements of the student and specialist in literature. All but the most obvious titles to which I allude are translated at least once into English.

It is a pleasure for me to record my gratitude to the Committee on Summer Faculty Fellowships at the University of Virginia for the grant that enabled me to complete the writing of this book. I also wish to thank Professor Joseph-M. Carrière for reading the entire manuscript.

Grateful acknowledgment is made to the University of Nebraska Press for authorizing me to quote from Gwendolyn Bay's *The Orphic Vision;* to the Johns Hopkins Press for permission to cite a paragraph from Georges Poulet's *The Interior Distance;* and to the Harvard University Press for allowing me to include a passage from Maurice Shroder's *Icarus: The Image of the Artist in French Romanticism.*

ROBERT T. DENOMMÉ

Charlottesville, Virginia
September 17, 1967

Nineteenth-Century
French Romantic Poets

1

Toward a Definition of Romanticism

Nineteenth-century French Romanticism emerged as
a sweeping rejection of the rational equilibrium such
as was proposed and interpreted by the eighteenth-
century *philosophes*. The leading exponents of the
Enlightenment maintained that a satisfactory explanation of man's predicament could be achieved through
the controlled processes of the individual's reasoning
powers. They founded their relativist interpretation of
the universe upon an empirical method of inquiry.
Their conclusions understandably emphasized the
practical rather than the abstract considerations in
man's condition. A meaningful sense of unity, order,
and harmony could be realized through the practical
and convenient adjustment of man's reason to external experience. The advocates of this attitude were, of
course, distrustful of the roles assigned the imagination and intuition, and most were agreed that reason
should exercise rigid control over man's other faculties. Voltaire took the view that the imagination
served only to stir the emotions and to encourage man
to engage in idle contemplation; Candide's final reaction to Pangloss' abstract musing stated the case co-
gently: "All of that is well and good, but we must
cultivate our garden." [1] The angel Jesrad advises the
beleaguered Zadig in equally plain language concerning the unravelled metaphysics contained in the problem of good and evil: "If there existed only good and
no evil in the world, this earth would be another earth,

the train of events would emanate from another order of wisdom, and that order, which would be perfect, can only exist there where the Supreme Being resides, and which no evil can touch." [2] The pragmatic thesis encountered in *Zadig* and *Candide* was the one most visibly adopted by the majority of *philosophes*.

By and large, the writers of the Enlightenment felt that too great an insistence upon the function of the imagination in the cognitive process could impair man's rational powers to the extent of reducing his ability to act with common sense. To a degree, the objection raised by some of the eighteenth-century thinkers reiterated Plato's earlier reservation concerning the disposition of responsibility entrusted to men who allowed themselves to be motivated primarily by inspiration. It will be remembered that Plato considered the imagination an uncontrollable faculty, too far removed from actual experience for it to be of any practical use in his *Republic*.[3] The inspired man, the poet, could not be relied upon to carry out matters of state because of his unpredictable nature. Therefore, poets such as Homer were conveniently dismissed from the Republic since they could not be expected to engage in the kinds of strategy required in the elaboration of the state. If it can be said that the *philosophes* of the Enlightenment undermined the structure of the Old Regime with their theses on relativity and their emphasis on material progress, it must be asserted that their method of argument, for the most part, relied more heavily upon factual than abstract considerations. The forcefulness of Montesquieu's social and political criticism in *L'Esprit des Lois* (*The Spirit of Laws*), for instance, is in no small way attributable to the calm and deliberate nature of its presentation. We readily discern that his conclusions are drawn from established facts and experience. Montesquieu's concern was identical to that of the other writers of the eighteenth century: the reform and reorganization of the social institutions responsible for ensuring the well-being of the French people. The writers of the Enlightenment sought first of all to expose the glaring inadequacies of the existent status quo, and to accomplish this aim, they enlisted only those arguments that were the exclusive product of reason and observation. In a sense, the philosophical tales, the essays and the thesis dramas which constitute the literary mainstream of the Age of Reason, encouraged the view that man's intelligence alone would suffice in solving the most pressing enigmas of the universe. Just as the orthodox critics of the seventeenth century called attention to the artist's workmanship at the expense of his inspiration, so did the majority of the *philosophes* underscore the logical ordering of art to the neglect of real lyricism. The classical age and the Enlightenment were conspicuously deficient in the kind of literary works that betrayed the enthusiasm and inspiration of the imagination. The Cartesian rationalism motivating the official critical pronouncements of Boileau adroitly bolstered the status quo of the political and religious orthodoxy of his time, thus serving as a convenient form of censorship. The *philosophes*, however, only voiced their distrust of the imagination because of its unsuitability as an effective weapon of reform.

By their insistence upon simplicity and natural law as the only acceptable bases for the new ethical code, the writers of the Enlightenment indirectly paved the way for French Romanticism.[4] The *philosophes* invited the individual to visualize a new society stripped of its complex trappings when they articulated their repeated criticisms of the arbitrariness of existing customs and conventions. Rousseau's *Le Contrat Social* (*The Social Contract*) articulates a vision of such a society: a pliable yet uncomplicated compromise entered into among men compelled by necessity and circumstance to live together in community. To a large extent, the presence of the lush exoticism permeating the novels of Jean-Jacques Rousseau and Bernardin de Saint-Pierre emerges as an explicit criticism of the conditions contaminating organized society in the eighteenth century. Both Rousseau and Bernardin de Saint-Pierre identify the ideal state of man with primitivism when confronted by a state of civilization which to them only corrodes and vilifies the individual's natural instincts. Both writers reject the view popular with the *philosophes* that it is necessary to define the individual with relationship and reference to the external world about him. For Bernardin de Saint-Pierre at least, wisdom and happiness are goals best realized in the primitive surroundings of exotic islands. Indeed, the fictional protagonist of his novel, *Paul et Virginie* (*Paul and Virginia*), proceeds relatively unimpaired in his quest for peace and contentment until he becomes victimized in the end by the cruel and unrelenting arbitrariness of social convention. Paul's ultimate compromise with society serves as his undoing. The lyrical novels of Rousseau and Bernardin de Saint-Pierre are considered preromantic precisely because their protagonists refuse to abide within the confines of any given social contexts. The exoticism encountered in their novels surrounds and enshrines the individual as he turns his back upon a deficient society which he regards as intolerable and unworthy of reform. Voltaire's fictional characters exhibit a more reverent attitude towards society even though they are bitterly critical of most of its customs and conventions. The naïve goodness and idealism of Zadig and Candide, for example, are eventually tempered with a practical widsom when they are jolted by the arbitrary demands of complex societies. In a sense, Voltaire's characters emerge as reluctant pragmatists; because of the attendant evils and injustices in existing social structures, they ultimately learn to adjust their enthusiasm and imagination to their practical reasoning power. Zadig and Candide learn from experience because they willingly confront it; their extracted wisdom in the end is the result of their constructive attitude toward social systems badly in need of reform. If the fictional heroes of Rousseau and Bernardin de Saint-Pierre preserve their idealistic stance, it is because they choose to remain, for the most part, oblivious to the obvious external organization about them.

It is no exaggeration to say that the exoticism in the novels of Rousseau and Bernardin de Saint-Pierre acts as a liberating force upon the protagonists who categorically exempt themselves from any real concern with the problems associated with social institutions. Left alone to primitive nature, Julie d'Etanges and Saint-Preux, for instance, consult only their instincts and emotions in order to satisfy their aspirations. When not contained by any remnant of convention, they express themselves in language more attuned to the inspiration of the imagination than controlled and tempered by reason. It is only when the cruel interpretation of petty class distinctions and prejudices imposes itself in the novel that their happiness and freedom come to an abrupt and tragic end. *La Nouvelle Héloïse* (*The Second Heloise*) is a novel that unfolds the basic conflicts between nature and society. As such, this epistolary work resembles many of the writings of the *philosophes* in that it points out the serious lack of balance between man's search for lasting and meaningful values and his actual status in the community of men. Both the rationalist thinkers of the Enlightenment and the preromantic writers of the latter part of the century advocated a drastic change in the status quo. The former believed that an adequate definition of man could be achieved through controlled reason and logic; the latter suggested that reason alone was incapable of arriving at a comprehensive understanding of man in the universe. Both the rationalists and the preromanticists looked hopefully to the French Revolution which they had prepared for the solutions which they sought. With the Revolution and the destruction of the Old Regime, it remained for the articulate man to fashion a new order and restore the lost equilibrium. The history of the attempts to achieve such objectives is in a real sense the story of French Romanticism.

To a very significant degree, the spirit of the Enlightenment underscored man's isolation from God. As Jean Cassou points out: "The *philosophes* taught man that he was ultimately alone, left to cultivate his own garden the best way he could." [5] His own powers of reason and observation appeared to be the only reassurance that he needed; progress and knowledge were the product of judicious reasoning and seasoned observation of social facts. Whatever confidence he enjoyed, however, was short-lived, for the French Revolution not only succeeded in overthrowing the old social and political order but the ensuing Industrial Revolution managed to destroy whatever vestiges of balance remained. Indeed, the upheaval caused by the two revolutions was of such breathtaking proportions that it bequeathed to the first generations of the nineteenth century an almost overwhelming sense of inadequacy and defeat. Before the onslaught of events that succeeded one another in rapid succession, it soon became evident that the equilibrium maintained in the Enlightenment had become woefully outdated, and had to be discarded. The plain fact was that the social and industrial revolutions intervened with such force in France that they nearly completely dislodged the scale of values to which the people had grown accustomed. Bewildered, the individual's consternation only increased as he witnessed the constantly shifting moods of the succeeding regimes and the wholesale adoption of so many conflicting makeshift values. The new society that emerged in the aftermath of the Revolution failed to provide the people with the kind of stable leadership and direction they expected. The truth of the matter was that the old equilibrium had been destroyed and had not been replaced with a new and acceptable one. If the Napoleonic campaigns at first won the enthusiasm of the younger generations, the fall of the empire in 1814 only inspired them with an abject sense of defeat and humiliation. With the eventual restoration of the Bourbon dynasty in 1815, the once ardent participants in the revolution felt that they had only been bequeathed broken promises of freedom and justice. The feelings of dissatisfaction and disillusionment that overtook them became so widespread that they became codified into what is known as the *mal du siècle*. In their frustration, an overwhelming number of survivors expressed their contempt for the easy rationalistic formulas which they had inherited from the *philosophes* of the preceding century. The anguish they experienced was articulated instead by a young writer whose published letter of 31 December 1799 crystallized the young romantics' search for meaning and understanding.

> Creator of light, forgive us our first errors! If we were so unfortunate as to misunderstand you in the century now ending, know that you will not have ushered us into the new century in vain. For it has resounded for us like the lightning of your thunder. . . . Lord, know that henceforth we shall praise you with the prophet. We beg you to accept this first hymn of praise to you during this last night of the century that enters into your eternity.[6]

Chateaubriand's prayer verbalized the fundamental reaction of the first generation of Romantics who, like him, sensed that the single-dimensional inheritance of the Enlightenment was incapable of piercing through the essential truths of the universe. The passionate fervor of his letter, moreover, set the tone for the type of renewal that was sought. Thanks to the irresistible intervention of history, the writers of the early nineteenth century would be afforded the opportunity of implementing their own methodologies in their respective pursuits and establishment of more acceptable and permanent equilibriums.

The disenchanted survivors of the Revolution required, however, the kinds of literary expression that were capable of reflecting their own fears and preoccupations. They had just emerged from the Revolution scathed by the bitter realization that their utopian dreams for the future had come to a sudden and abortive end. They expressed their own disgust and dissatisfaction with the evolved political and social establishments by withdrawing into an escapist world of reverie through their imaginations. What interested them particularly were works that stimulated the imagination and the emotions. They would eventually create their own Romantic literature, but in the meantime, they availed themselves of foreign works that had enjoyed a certain vogue in France since the latter part of the eighteenth century. Far from being an exclusively French phenomenon, Romanticism was rather a European movement that already had exercised a far-reaching effect upon English and German literature. Because of the somewhat cosmopolitan nature of the Enlightenment, the novels of Richardson, filled with pity and compassion, and the poetical works of Gray, permeated with a serene melancholy, made their way into France, and enjoyed a certain popularity among those who were now dismissing the more abstract intellectual discussions as futile and insipid. Moreover, there coexisted with the rationalist *philosophes* of the eighteenth century such preromantic writers as Rousseau, Marivaux, Bernardin de Saint-Pierre, and the abbé Prévost who generously sprinkled their works with the elements of sentiment and emotion that were sought by the young French readers of the nineteenth century. In the wake of the Revolution, the disillusioned sensibilities of Chateaubriand's generation were assuaged by the melancholic charm emanating from the poetic landscape evocations of the Scottish poet, Ossian (Mac Pherson), who enjoyed considerable vogue in the first decades of the new century. The more desperate advocates of the *mal du siècle,* found an articulate "hero" in the translation of Goethe's novel, *Werther.* In a word, the official and conventional publications of such tepid neo-classical writers as Legouvé and Chênedollé were either maligned or ignored by those who claimed a need for a personal literature. The desire to sever all links with the immediate past led them eventually to admire Lord Byron's bold defiance of social conventions and to appreciate the Spanish *romanceros* which projected the imagination back into the Middle Ages.

It would be a serious error to assume that the Romantic effusions of the English and continental writers won the wholehearted attention and support of literary France. It has already been noted that Romanticism emerged as a somewhat tardy movement in France when compared with England and Germany. The spirit of Classicism and of the pseudo neo-Classicism that dominated French literature for more than two centuries was destined logically to win the ready approval of the imperial regime of Napoleon and the restored Bourbon dynasty which lasted until 1830. In spite of his own predilection for the verse of Ossian, Napoleon was anxious to promote a literary revival which incorporated the rules and formulas of the orthodox classical school, presumably because it would safeguard the traditional association of Crown and Church. The expression of emotion and sentiment prevalent in the works of the early Romanticists was considered a brazen innovation, and consequently viewed with suspicion by regimes understandably eager to conserve or restore certain ingredients of the prerevolutionary status quo. A strict censorship was instituted during Napoleon's administration that favored the publication of odes, tragedies, and novels written according to classical prescriptions, thus keeping the more radical literature of the Romanticists in check. The unrelenting resistance of the official and conservative factions gradually compelled the young writers to organize themselves in workshops or *céna-*

cles, as they were called, in order to define their own views with some kind of precision. These meetings may very well account for the fact that the esthetics of French Romanticism is the most effective combination of the use of reason and emotion. Apart from preserving the French writers from the extremes of the German Romanticists and the excesses of their English counterparts, these unofficial laboratories endowed French Romanticism with a sense of cohesiveness that was to endure until 1830 when the Romantic battle was finally won.

Imbued with the liberal ideas contained in Montesquieu's *L'Esprit des Lois,* Madame de Staël emerged as the first significant theorist of French Romanticism with the publication of her book of essays in 1800 entitled *De la Littérature considérée dans ses rapports avec les institutions sociales (Concerning Literature and its Relationships with Social Institutions).* Despite her enthusiastic approval of the French Revolution, Madame de Staël was suspected by the Directory of 1792, and was looked upon with disfavor by Napoleon during his reign, thus obliging her to seek refuge at Coppet on Lake Geneva and in her estate in the outskirts of metropolitan Paris. Nevertheless, Madame de Staël exerted considerable influence among the young writers of the time because of the intellectual *avant-garde* tinge in her views on Romanticism. Her drawing rooms at Coppet and on the rue de Grenelle in Paris during the Restoration served as a haven for such aspiring writers as Benjamin Constant and Chateaubriand who were able to air their liberal ideas on literature and politics.

More directly influenced by the rationalist strain of the Enlightenment rather than by the lyrical tenor of the pre-Romanticist writers, Madame de Staël utilized Montesquieu's thesis on the relativity of laws and customs as her central argument in *De la Littérature.* In underscoring the need for a new and personal literature for France, she reaffirmed the *philosophes'* principle concerning the limitless perfectibility of the human mind. But the requisite for human and social progress is political freedom. The history of such progress points out the relativity of social institutions. Various types of literatures depend upon variety in countries, climates, and societies. Beauty, then, is something relative to internal conditions. The laws and codes that define and dictate works of art are at best fragile and arbitrary. More than anything else, literary works betray the heart and mind of a given time and a given nation. To illustrate her thesis, Madame de Staël classifies all of western literature as either northern literature or southern literature.[7] Northern literature (that of Britain and Germany), she goes on to explain, finds much of its inspiration in the fog of those countries; it considers the imagination and dreams important, and if it does not always translate faithfully the spirit of Christianity, it always betrays some kind of religiosity. By contrast, southern literature (that of Greece and Rome, Italy, France, and Spain) is influenced both by the sunny climates of the countries and by paganism. It is the kind of literature that submits itself readily to the dictates of reason alone. As a logical corollary to her thesis, Madame de Staël reminds the French people of their present predicament by bluntly asserting that new societies need new literatures. The new literature that France seeks must be able to fulfill the needs and aspirations of a nation torn from within as a result of the French Revolution. "At the time in which we live, melancholy serves as the real inspiration of poetic talent."[8] Despite its apparent unevenness, many of its presumptuous conclusions and its numerous summary judgments, *De la Littérature* was considered the first important critical treatise on the French Romantic movement. Writers as important as Stendhal and Victor Hugo came to regard Madame de Staël's work as a kind of manifesto from which they borrowed ideas and arguments to evolve their respective literary creeds.

What mattered most to the young generation of readers who accepted *De la Littérature* as the official cornerstone of their thinking was the fact that Madame de Staël managed so convincingly to crystallize the formula of the romantic mind with such declarations as: "Whatever greatness man achieves, he owes it to the painful realization that his destiny will always remain uncompleted." [9]

A short while before the three volumes which constitute *De l'Allemagne (Concerning Germany)* were scheduled for publication in Paris, Madame de Staël in an ill-advised move sent a copy of the completed proofs to the Emperor. The letter accompanying the manuscript made it clear that she sought Napoleon's approbation and that she wished to return to his good graces. The latter's reaction to her overtures was as drastic as it was unexpected: *De l'Allemagne* was ordered pulped, the printer's copy was seized and destroyed, and the author was banished from France. Thus, the French publication of the book was delayed until 1814, although the 1810 manuscript was published in London in 1813. The obvious incompatibility of the political climate of the imperial regime with the general tenor of *De l'Allemagne* doubtlessly accounted for the ban put on it in 1810. To a degree, Madame de Staël's treatise may be interpreted as a kind of wholesale tribute to the German nation even though such was not the primary objective of the author.

Whatever else, *De l'Allemagne* bespeaks its author's genuine enthusiasm for the writings of Schiller, Goethe, and Schlegel which she had discovered during a recent trip to Germany. The book is divided into four major sections, the first three of which may be considered as a rather subjective study of the character and temperament of the German people and a somewhat stimulating though uneven appraisal of their literature. The last part, by far the most important of the four, entitled "Religion and Enthusiasm," unfolds the essential thesis of the entire work. Madame de Staël defines "enthusiasm" and the profound mysticism which she sees in the German nation. This mysticism, she adds, accounts for the impressive display of energy of the people in their untiring quest for knowledge and in their desire to be free. "Enthusiasm" provides the people with the kind of constructive impetus that is needed for them to persevere in their goals. The acquisition of the same kind of impetus is what Madame de Staël believes is needed to inspire the oppressed people of other lands to struggle for the achievement of their own national unity.

In her appeals for greater freedom and expansiveness in French literature, Madame de Staël voices her contempt for Classicism and neo-Classicism in clear and unmistakable language. France must begin to look at the literary expression of other countries, notably that of Germany, in order that the horizons of French literature may be broadened. The tone of her exhortations were certain to draw the applause of the young survivors of the Revolution who had been clamoring for the kinds of work that could translate the anguish and dissatisfaction which they felt: "We can experience more profound emotions in the reading of works much less ordered and contrived than ours; foreign plays are sometimes more striking and bolder than French plays, and often, foreign plays are endowed with some unknown power that speaks directly to the heart and comes nearest in approximating the emotions that bestir us."[10] Through their perusal of German literature, Madame de Staël continues, the French will discover a new type of literature, Romantic literature. Paradoxically, the study of this German Romanticism will induce the French to rediscover the roots of their own literature, and thus allow them to establish a truly indigenous body of artistic expression:

Ancient literature is for us moderns a transplanted literature; however, romantic or chivalrous literature is indigenous to us, since it is our own religion and institutions that have inspired it.

Romantic literature alone is capable of further improvement because it stems from our own soil and character. Consequently, it is the only type of literature that is able to grow and renew itself. It expresses our religion, it recalls our history: its origins may be traced to the Middle Ages but not to Antiquity.[11]

The essential characteristics of Romantic literature in Madame de Staël's estimation are its spirituality and its Christianity. More than any other religion perhaps, Christianity has always served as a vital source of inspiration. Indeed, there exists a close proximity between poetic and religious sentiment: "Above all, religious and poetic sentiment within us makes us conscious of the Divinity that resides in us. Poetry is the language most natural to all religions." [12] Moreover, the enigma of human destiny is forever impressed upon the imagination of the poet which inspires him with the courage and boldness necessary to relate the spectacle of man. Madame de Staël's insistence upon the important function of the imagination and inspiration in poetry ran counter to the established tenets of Classicism and Rationalism alike, and her thesis was considered tantamount to a categorical repudiation of the literature produced in France during the seventeenth and eighteenth centuries. Rather than draw his messages from the ordered social world outside himself, the poet was now being encouraged to search deeply within himself in order to extract the sentiments imprisoned in his soul which would allow him to express with moving eloquence the nature of the human condition. Thus, the poet's genius could not afford to be hampered by any restrictions of an outdated code for fear that the resulting poetry resemble the didactic and circumstantial verse of the classical French writers: "Rules are nothing but the guidebooks of talent; they merely inform us that Corneille, Racine, and Voltaire consulted them. But if we manage to obtain our objectives, why bother to quarrel about methods? Isn't the objective [of literature] to move the soul and ennoble it?" [13] Madame de Staël's concluding statement in *De l'Allemagne* exhorts French poets to steep themselves in the study of German literature because it betrays the type of genuine love of nature, the arts and philosophy which break away from the restrictions and formulas that dominate Southern literatures.

Madame de Staël reveals her adeptness as an effective theorist in *De l'Allemagne* in spite of her somewhat colorless style devoid of practically all imagery. Her treatise demonstrates a remarkable ability to capture the sometimes vague considerations on the role of sentiment and emotion in literature in quasi-aphoristic language. In emphasizing the social and political aspects in the history of French literature, she reflects the liberal heritage bequeathed her by the rationalist exponents of the French Enlightenment. Yet her thesis that modern literature must be poetic in its expression, national in its inspiration, chivalrous as to its sources and christian in its essence was to an extent the formal and theoretical crystallization of the themes and attitudes that had already been utilized by another innovator of nineteenth-century literature, Alphonse de Chateaubriand.

Despite his professed admiration for the cult of classical beauty and his negative reaction to what he termed "the excesses of individualism," [14] Chateaubriand was hailed as one of the first spokesmen for the new and ardent generation of the first decades of the nineteenth century. Surrounded by an admiring coterie that included such notable figures as Ballanche, the selfstyled Christian Plato, and Senancour, the mystical dreamer,[15] Chateaubriand had returned to France in 1800 after having served briefly in the army of *émigrés*. His first major publication, *Essai historique sur les Révolutions*, was an attempt to explain the French Revolution by revolutions that had preceded it. His thesis, "that there is nothing new under the sun, and that one finds in old as well as in new revolutions the same kind of figures and attitudes encountered in the French Revolution," appeared as a blatant contradiction of Montesquieu's earlier affirmation on the principle of human progress. The essay suggests the confusion residing in Chateaubriand's mind between the rationalist strain he inherited from the eighteenth-century Encyclopedists and a deep-rooted concern for religion which had overtaken him even before the death of his mother in 1798. What is decidedly manifest in this one-volume essay are the lyrical effusions that become frequently injected into main arguments of the thesis. There is more ardor and enthusiasm than there is clarity in his presentation; interpolations of such things as long evocations of primitive American nature scenes intrude seriously upon the factual evidence offered in support of his views. If the *Essai historique sur les révolutions* may be considered as the admission of Chateaubriand's religious doubt, then, the publication of his monumental *Le Génie du Christianisme* (*The Genius of Christianity*), published in 1802, must be hailed as his affirmation of faith.

The fusion of fact with lyricism already in evidence in Chateaubriand's essay on the history of revolutions receives a more sustained application in the five-volume treatise on Christianity which was conveniently published in France just four days prior to the proclamation of Napoleon's Concordat with the Church on 18 April 1802. As an apology for the Christian religion, *Le Génie du Christianisme* represents a radical departure from the methodology hitherto deemed appropriate in the history of apologetics. Chateaubriand's objectives are perhaps best explained in his own terms: ". . . to call upon all the enchantment of the imagination and all interests of the human heart to come to the aid of this religion against which they [the *philosophes* of the Enlightenment] have taken up arms." [16] Despite its tenuous position as a valid defense of religion, the fact remains that *Le Génie du Christianisme* was hailed as an outstanding publication by the surviving generations of the Revolution who had disavowed their allegiance to the rationalistic principles of the Enlightenment. Eager themselves to express their faith, hope, and love in some principle, they readily abandoned any critical stance when they accepted the author's prefatory statement as a valid criterion for belief: "J'ai pleuré et j'ai cru" ("I cried and I believed"). Many of the conclusions asserted in *Le Génie du Christianisme* will appear specious to the modern reader, who will notice some of the obvious flaws in the author's dialectical presentation. For example, in his argument that the classical writers of Antiquity witnessed nature only indirectly through mythology, Chateaubriand appears to ignore the genuinely effective nature evocations of Lucretius, Vergil, Theocritus, or Horace, and consequently invalidates much of his own argument. His apology for the Christian religion, however, was meant to appeal to the reader's sensibilities; in awakening his feelings for nature, Chateaubriand hoped to awaken in him predispositions that would lead to reverie, meditation, and communication with the Divinity. This accounts for the interspersing of so many nature descriptions after the completion of his main lines of argument. Indeed, the inclusion of such elaborate nature evocations was intended to illustrate the points made in his impressive treatise. If *Le Génie du Christianisme* was hailed as the major key work of the opening decades of the nineteenth century, it was because it contained most of the major themes and techniques that would be taken up and exploited by the later Romanticists. Unlike Madame de Staël who argued for literary innovation with social and political considerations, Chateaubriand claimed that the new literary expression received its impetus from man's unending quest for spiritual meaning. In Chateaubriand's estimation, the

Christian religion was the superior cult because it har-
bored the most beauty and the greatest excellence and
these were proofs of its divinity.

The incorporation of both literary theory and practice in *Le Génie du Christianisme* provided the kind
of codification that was sought by the exponents of
innovation in literary expression. Chateaubriand's
theoretical discussions enjoyed the benefit of practical
illustration. A case in point was the insertion, after
1805, of the semi-autobiographical narrative, *René*, in
explanation of the author's conception of *le vague des
passions* and the *mal du siècle*, notions that were destined to enjoy a popular vogue in the literature of the
nineteenth century. But as we have noted, what particularly distinguishes the literary theory of Chateaubriand is its close association with the spiritual elements that underscore the major tenets of the Christian religion. In their advocacy of material progress,
the majority of the *philosophes* of the Enlightenment
considered organized religion and metaphysical contemplation detrimental and obstructive manifestations. They pleaded rather for a practical philosophy
of life stripped of all useless metaphysical concern.
The history of Christianity, they pointed out, was the
shameful account of unjust wars and persecutions that
only obstructed the advancement of man's progress.
Chateaubriand's considerable success in restoring
Christianity as an institution capable of endowing
man's life with new meaning was in no small way due
to the historical moment during which his apologia
appeared. Whatever else it accomplished, the French
Revolution had broken with the past and left its
young survivors bewildered and dissatisfied in a world
bereft of the more obvious lasting values. Chateaubriand's spiritual message was a timely one.

The author's attack on Classicism and neo-Classicism begins with a ringing denunciation of the apparent contradiction of Christian France's adoption of an
essentially pagan literature. Therein lies the major cul-

tural problem besetting modern France, he continues in his preface. Bequeathed only seriously outdated ideals by Antiquity, it becomes necessary to turn to Christianity as a more genuine source of inspiration.

In the second part of the apology, "The Poetics of Christianity," Chateaubriand explains that the poetics of modern literature is deeply rooted in the mysteries of the Christian religion.

> How much more favored [than the poet of Antiquity] is the Christian poet who in his solitude walks with God! Finally rid of this flock of absurd little gods who previously overran the forests, the woods are now filled with the all-encompassing Divinity. The gifts of prophesy and wisdom, mystery and religion—all seem to reside forever in their sacred depths.[17]

In the author's view, it is Christianity that inspires man to be affected by the spectacle of nature which in turn induces in him the *vague des passions*, in reality man's inarticulate nostalgia for God. This feeling of disgust and dissatisfaction experienced by the sensitive individual for the immediate world that surrounds him receives an elaborate treatment in the section entitled *René*.[18] *René* not only serves as an elucidation of the second part of *Le Génie du Christianisme* but it also advances the first definition of the *mal du siècle* which was destined to become one of the principal themes of Romanticism.

Despite the critic Sainte-Beuve's contention that René's plight had been described before by Vergil, St. Augustine, and Albert Dürer,[19] Chateaubriand describes the predicament of his protagonist within the context that made itself most readily understood by the readers of the early nineteenth century. *René* does more than merely define the special predicament of the individual who feels alienated from the society in which he finds himself: it also utilizes the language and techniques that will later become closely identified with the writings of such Romanticists as Lamartine, Hugo, and Vigny. The vague aspiration toward an ideal that is never clearly defined is what the disenchanted René experiences in his willful isolation from the society of men and their cities whose narrow limitations he cannot accept. The language employed by Chateaubriand in the description of his hero's reactions, his choice and juxtaposition of imagery betray the kind of poetic lyricism generally associated with the major French Romanticists. Such language, in fact, conveys a sense of distance from the usual preoccupations experienced by men who refer themselves to the external organizations in which they live. The disassociation which René achieves from his social environment allows him to pursue unhampered his own quest for meaning and value. The individualism of such Romantic heroes as René usually reveals itself by the use of language that is more often than not categorical and absolute.

> What I lacked was something that would fill the emptiness of my existence: I went down into the valley, I climbed the mountain, calling out with all the strength of my desire for the ideal object of a future love that would consume me; I embraced it in the winds, I thought I could hear it in the groaning of the stream; everything became identified with this phantom I had imagined, the stars in the sky, even the principle of life in the universe.[20]

The vagueness of expression in Chateaubriand's description of his protagonist's even vaguer conception of what he considers to be his ideal is certainly a far cry from the controlled and precise language used by the rationalistic exponents of the Enlightenment. Part of René's vagueness of expression results from his individualistic response to certain feelings and experiences; what he wishes to communicate is his inner response to these feelings and experiences which find no easy corroboration in the accepted world of facts. In his need to identify that which he experiences within himself with something outside himself, he comes to parallel his moods and feelings with such things as a dry leaf being swept away in the cold autumnal wind or with a single stone lying in some prairie. Chateaubriand's use of personification or of what Ruskin disparagingly termed *the pathetic fallacy* was to become one of the favorite devices of the later Romantic poets. The themes of otherness, isolation, and the sensitive individual misunderstood by the world in which he lives were all topics that would be taken up again and exploited by poets and prose writers during the reign of Romanticism in the nineteenth century.

More than anything else, however, Chateaubriand's autobiographical narrative articulated the widespread reaction of ennui which was shared by the survivors of the Revolution: "Alas! I remained alone, alone on earth! A secret languor overtook my body. I felt all the more strongly this disgust for life which I had experienced ever since my childhood. Gradually my heart ceased feeding my thoughts, and I was only cognizant of my existence through the profound sense of boredom that I felt." [21] *René*'s expression of total disgust and dissatisfaction with life such as he experienced it suggests the uncompromising attitude that would later characterize so many of the proposals of the social Romanticists of the 1830's and 1840's.

The third part of *Le Génie du Christianisme*, entitled "Religion, the Fine Arts and Literature," emphasized the close association between Christianity and all forms of artistic expression. The greatest themes in Western literature, continued Chateaubriand, owe a certain debt to the sense of the infinite which is derived from man's contemplation of his relationship to God. Christianity invites the individual to meditate on the spectacle of nature and to consider the flight of time at the sight of ruins, illustrating once again that it is a greater source of inspiration than Greek mythology.

More perhaps through his practice of literature in such works as *Atala* and *René* than by the elaborate elucidation of his theories in *Le Génie du Christianisme,* Chateaubriand exerted an influence of considerable importance on the development of modern literary aesthetics. His forceful repudiation of the rules that had for so long restrained classical and neo-classical expression, and his convincing condemnation of ancient mythology as an ineffective vehicle for the upsurging modern spirit of post-revolutionary France did much to foster the kind of liberal atmosphere that eventually would permit and encourage the free development of French letters. In emphasizing the poetic values contained in the Bible and in the Christian religion, he prompted his countrymen to re-evaluate their national cultural heritage which they hitherto so readily dismissed as inconsequential and inferior. In underscoring the great artistic merit in the Gothic cathedrals of medieval France, he kindled his readers' sense of history. His study of the sentiment of moral solitude in *René* gave form to the French attitude that allowed for comparison with that provided in Goethe's *Werther.*

The emotional crisis in post-revolutionary France suffered by those who had identified their hopes and aspirations with the aims of the great upheaval found its fullest expression in the literary innovations that were advocated by such writers as Chateaubriand and Madame de Staël. By and large, however, the movement that was destined to liberate the writers from the restrictions imposed by a long classical tradition was prevented from asserting itself until the 1820's. The sustained and vociferous resistance of conservative forces eventually induced the advocates of the new literature to seek some kind of unity among themselves. The first significant attempts at organization resulted in the establishment of two groups of writers whose political and religious views cast them at least temporarily as conservatives and liberals. Such conservatives as Hugo and Vigny joined forces with the two brothers Emile and Antony Deschamps to define their position in the recently-founded journal, *Le Conservateur littéraire*, and eventually in *La Muse française*. In 1824, they rallied in the drawing rooms of Charles Nodier, librarian at the Arsenal, where they formed the first official laboratory or *cénacle* of Romanticism. With their penchant for Rationalism and their admitted preference for prose as the most effective form of literary expression, the liberal counterpart of the *cénacle* group, consisting of such notable writers as Stendhal, Ludovic Vitet and Sainte-Beuve, asserted their anti-classical attitudes in *Le Globe* and through such brutal assaults upon traditionalist sentiment as Stendhal's *Racine et Shakespeare* in 1823.

If the idea of a literary revolution took so long in enlisting the enthusiasm of its likely adherents, it was doubtlessly due to the confusion that distracted the various leaders of the revolt. The truth of the matter was that there appeared to be less expressed opposition between the classicists and the romanticists than between the conservative and the liberal factions. The conservative writers of the *cénacle* were in a sense somewhat classical by their avowed allegiance to the traditional monarchy, yet they professed their contempt for the neo-classical attitudes of Voltaire and stated their preference for the romantic writings of Chateaubriand. By the same ironic twist, the liberal exponents tended toward classical attitudes such as they were expressed by the rationalist *philosophes* of the Enlightenment, yet they were eager to champion the cause of Romanticism out of their love and admiration for freedom of thought and expression.

For lack of any cohesive doctrine or program, the Romanticists experienced considerable difficulty in avoiding conflicting and contradictory statements in their repudiations of the verbal accusations brought forth by their detractors. The desired merger between the liberal and conservative exponents of French Romanticism was accomplished mainly through the efforts of Victor Hugo in 1827 who had recently evolved to liberalism with the publication of his *Ode à la Colonne de 1827* (*Ode to the Column of 1827*). The reconciliation between Hugo and Sainte-Beuve incited both factions within the Romantic movement to unite under the leadership of the former in his drawing room at the rue Notre-Dame-des-Champs. This second *cénacle* aimed at resolving the differences that prevented the Romanticists from campaigning effectively against their conservative rivals in the French Academy who had branded them as outlaws and who vowed to prevent them from flourishing. The year 1827 may be called a turning point for the young Romanticists who had become united under the tutelage of Victor Hugo. Two important publications of manifesto-making proportions turned the tide for the young writers who were waging a relentless battle for recognition and acceptance. The *Préface de Cromwell* (*Preface to Cromwell*) by Hugo and the *Tableau historique et critique de la poésie française et du théâtre français au XVIe siècle* (*Historical and Critical Survey of French Poetry and Theatre during the 16th-Century*) by Sainte-Beuve are remarkable attempts to define French Romanticism in both a modern and historical context. Hugo's *Préface* was a formulation of doctrine for the new writers, while Sainte-Beuve's *Tableau* was a study in rapprochement between the lyrical and dramatic inspiration of the Renaissance and of the nineteenth century.

Taking the Romantic battle to the theatre, Hugo meant his *Préface de Cromwell* to serve as the constitution for the Romanticists' creed. Presented as "general considerations on art and aesthetics," the *Préface de Cromwell* concentrates upon the problem of modern drama, yet most of the conclusions arrived at by Hugo contain a certain relevance to the theory and practice of poetry. The main thesis entertained in the *Préface de Cromwell* is that the combination of what is termed the *sublime* with the *grotesque* produces man's most complete vision of reality. Hugo establishes his premise for the sublime and the grotesque upon the notion that Christianity induces man to portray man completely: body and spirit, shadow and light. In a sense, Hugo's point of departure for the literary theory that he expounds in the *Préface de Cromwell* bears an uncanny similarity to motivating principles in the theories of Madame de Staël and Chateaubriand:

> Christianity brings truth to poetry. Like it, modern poetry will see things all at once and comprehensively. It will begin to realize that everything in creation is not humanly beautiful, that beauty exists next to ugliness, that the grotesque is the opposite of the sublime. . . . Poetry, finally, will begin to imitate nature, to blend in its creations, without, however, confusing them, shadow and light, the sublime and the grotesque, in other words, the body and the soul, the animalistic and the spiritual. There is the principle that is unknown to Antiquity: a new type will be introduced in poetry, and this type is called the grotesque.[22]

What is particularly interesting in Hugo's theory of the sublime and the grotesque is his claim that the right combination of these two elements constitutes our best view and interpretation of reality. As a theory of reality, there is an admitted plausibility in Hugo's conception. Yet his insistence upon the apparent juxtaposition of these elements to one another contradicts his claim that they should be made to fuse together. In maintaining the view that the fullness of poetic expression resides in the romantic conception of drama, Hugo is moved to explain: "The poetry of Christianity, the real poetry of our time is then the drama, for the true character of drama is the real. Reality results quite naturally from the combination of two types, the sublime and the grotesque, which intersect in drama just as their intersection is evident in life and creation. For true poetry, complete poetry is to be found in the harmonious blend of opposites." [23] Yet his own recurrent use of such expressions as: beauty and ugliness, light and shadow, mind and body, all suggest more the impression of antithesis and contrast than they do the "harmonious blend" that he advocates in the *Préface de Cromwell*. Whatever may have been the impression conveyed to his readers in 1827, *Hernani* and the poetry that followed in 1830 underscored Hugo's marked predilection for contrasts and antitheses. In this regard, at least, it may be said that the author's own poetic practice constitutes a somewhat radical evolution from the position that had been maintained in the *Préface de Cromwell*. Indeed, the technique of antithesis, so characteristic of the thought and style of the Romanticists, received its thorough initiation in the numerous writings of Victor Hugo.

Whatever may be contended concerning Hugo's theory of the sublime and the grotesque, the *Préface de Cromwell* did emerge as a forceful statement of the aims and the philosophy of the new writers. Hugo's categorical opposition to rules and restrictions in literary expression is underlined in blunt but unequivocal language:

> Freedom in art! . . . There are no rules other than the general rules underlying human nature. Let us take the hammer to the theories, the poetics and the systems. Let us remove all the old plaster that masks the façade of art. Whatever rules must exist are special to each work of art and result from the conditions that enable the work to see the light of day.[24]

The *Préface de Cromwell* led logically to the publication and performances of Hugo's drama, *Hernani* in February of 1830. The battle of the French Romanticists with the traditionalist factions in French society scored an uncontested victory with the stormy yet ultimate acceptance of the play by the public. With their integration into the mainstream of society, the young writers who united under the leadership of Hugo and Sainte-Beuve in the second *cénacle* began to assert their talent and originality in divergent ways and forms. Moreover the individualism that dictated the underlying principle of the Romanticists called for the dispersal of the members of the *cénacle* as soon as it became evident that there remained no further need for organization.

The literary revolution effected by the performances of *Hernani* in February and the political upheaval of July of the same year emerged as eloquent reminders that France had evolved somewhat dramatically since the Restoration of 1815. If the year 1830 marked an end in the struggle for recognition and official accept- ance for the Romanticists, it also ushered in a new era for the writers who had finally succeeded in supplant- ing lingering neo-classical attitudes. The confusion that arose from the effects of the French Revolution was further complicated by an encroaching Industrial Revolution that manifested itself in France as early as 1820. By 1830, the social fabric of France had changed radically with the emergence of a new class, the proletariat, a direct product of the industrializa- tion that transformed the major French cities. The at- tendant problems that beset such transformation elicited the enthusiastic commitment of economists, religious reformers, and politicians of all types to pro- grams intended to refashion the institutions of a na- tion whose equilibrium had been destroyed with the fall of the Old Regime. The majority of the young writers who hitherto had been content to describe their personal experiences in elegiac verses took to the political arena where they frequently asserted them- selves with the resoluteness of the most revolutionary advocates of social change. Soon, many of the publica- tions of the Romanticists reflected the excitement experienced in a society engaged in an intense search for new and vital direction. Poets such as Lamartine and Hugo expressed their concern to have the literature written by the Romanticists relate to the fundamental problems confronting the majority of their countrymen.

The French Romanticists who expressed a social concern asserted their views with such confidence and authority that it could only be directly derived from their own conception of their function as poets. As the selfappointed leaders of a society in pressing need of guidance, such writers as Lamartine, Hugo, and even Vigny pressed for reforms with the kind of messianic zeal which succeeded in making them strangely articulate. The sense of confidence and authority enjoyed by such writers stemmed in part from the conviction that their inspiration did set them apart since it was, as Madame de Staël and Chateaubriand had stated, a gift of God that rendered their vision of the world comprehensive. The recitation of the poet's creed by Vigny's protagonist, Stello, conveys the sense of assurance experienced by the Romantic poet:

> I believe in myself, because I feel a secret power at the bottom of my heart that is invisible and indefinable like a forewarning of the future and a revelation of the mysterious causes of our own time. I believe in myself, because there is not any beauty, any greatness, any harmony in nature which does not produce a prophetic shudder in me, which does not transmit a profound emotion in my entrails, or does not swell my eyelids with tears that are inexplicably divine. I am firmly convinced that I have been given some ineffable vocation. I believe it is so because of the limitless pity that is stirred in me by the sight of men, my companions in misery, and also because of the desire in me to extend to them a helping hand and to encourage them with appropriate words of love and commiseration.[25]

The profession of faith and self-assurance expressed by Stello translates rather adequately the mystical ingredient that may be found in many of the declarations made by the so-called social Romanticists during the July Monarchy of Louis-Philippe. Nor does the unrestrained nature of such admissions limit itself to the pronouncements of inspired poets; it permeates the style and thought of such thinkers as Saint-Simon, Enfantin, Lamennais, and Pierre Leroux who all sought to reshape the social, political, and religious institutions of nineteenth-century France.

To a considerable extent, French Romanticism may be defined by the exalted fervor and the messianic zeal that motivates the greater number of messages that it imparts. This same fervor and zeal accounts for much that may strike us to be absolute and categorical in the texts of the social Romanticists. Their humanitarian concern translates more directly their dreams of social utopias than it reflects any accurate appraisal of reality based upon the observation of facts. Since the writers concerned supposedly unfold to us their innermost revelations gotten from some omniscient power, the language in which they express themselves betrays a categorical refusal to temper or modify their messages in any way. Their adamant rejection of all compromise emanates from the ingrained conviction that their vision transcends experience and reality. Consequently, their proposals for social reform more often than not remain the fanciful elaboration of private ideologies.

That the position of the poet as leader and guide went virtually unchallenged during the 1830's and 1840's is indication enough of the state of ferment and confusion that beset the regime of Louis-Philippe. In the face of much hapless and baffling direction, the poet, like the radical social and religious reformers of the time, availed himself of the opportunity at hand to proclaim his new function as the true emancipator of the beleaguered masses. Irrespective of his effectiveness or ineffectiveness as a social adviser, the real fact of the matter was that the poet had evolved considerably from his unenviable status in Plato's republic to the respected position he now enjoyed as a social humanitarian. The mysticism and the metaphysical complexion that punctuated so much of the writing of the revolutionaries of the hour loomed as a sharp contrast to the calm and methodical reasoning that directed the arguments of the eighteenth-century *philosophes* in their efforts at reform. The social, political, religious, and poetical elements merged together to the extent that it became virtually impossible to ascertain which aspect dominated the struggle for liberation. Saint-Simon complicated his drive for a complete synthesis of modern society by injecting premises of a spiritual nature that only encouraged his disciple, Enfantin, to evolve his doctrines into an elaborate and confusing system of metaphysical socialism after 1825. In like manner, Lamennais' concerted attempt to link his radical social philosophy to a revolutionized Catholicism breathed the prophetic language of an Isaiah and presented a vision of the world that bordered on the hallucinatory. Into such a frame of reference, such major Romantic poets as Hugo, Lamartine, and Vigny elaborated their respective views on the function of the poet, which further projected the mentality that inspired the reforms of the social Romanticists.

Lamartine was the first of the Romantic poets to argue that poetry had a service to render society with the publication in 1831 of his "Ode sur les Révolutions" ("Ode on Revolutions"). In terms that predicted the statesmanlike qualities in the pronouncements of his subsequent political involvement, Lamartine issued a moving plea to the people requesting their commitment to the movements of history and urging their cooperation in furthering the struggle for progress. The prefatory essay to his complete works in 1834 clearly indicated his evolution from the type of idyllic evocations that characterized his earlier poetry; "Des Destinées de la poésie" ("Concerning the Destiny of Poetry") made it plain that Romantic poetry to be effective had to speak to the people of France in clear and simple language:

Henceforth, these popular geniuses [the poets] must concentrate all their efforts in making popular the truths derived from love, reason and the exalted emotions of religion and inspiration. This kind of poetry remains to be written: the times demand it, the people are hungry for it; they, in fact, are more instinctively poetic than we are, because they are closer to nature than we are. Yet they require someone who can interpret nature for them. It is for us to render service to them, to explain to them in terms understandable to them, all that which bespeaks the goodness, nobility, generosity, patriotism and the piety that God has placed in their hearts.[26]

The cautious faith and optimism emerging from Lamartine's poetic manifesto permitted him to achieve the kind of balance that endowed the greatest part of his poetry with the sense of calm and moderation that made it acceptable even to the stubborn neo-classical readers who lingered after 1830. It may be safely ventured to state that his personal and political views, often curiously conservative and liberal at the same time, enabled him to write Romantic poetry that maintained an equilibrium between personal enthusiasm and inspiration and the external world of fact and experience.

Victor Hugo's various personal responses to the social, political and religious attitudes that manifested themselves during the greater portion of the nineteenth-century account for his numerous and often contradictory statements concerning the function of Romantic poetry. Hugo's somewhat dramatic evolution from the conservatism and traditionalism of his youth to the liberal socialism of his later years was in no small measure attributable to the nature of his own experience and reaction. A study of the development of Hugo's poetical practices is to a large extent an examination of his life activity since both his theories and his poetry reflect his own experiences. This kind of transposition of personal experience into poetry and other art forms characterizes the publications of many of the French Romanticists and lends to their work the stamp of individualism that usually is associated with it. Consequently, some kind of direct or indirect reference to the life of the poet concerned is frequently required in any serious consideration of his poetic art since the two are more often than not inextricably interrelated.

The conventional and circumstantial tone that dominates Hugo's earliest efforts in poetry is in a sense justified by the favor that he enjoyed with neo-classical traditionalists and the pension that was granted to him by Louis XVIII. If Hugo later became attracted to the somewhat more radical aspects of Romanticism in the middle 1820's, it was because the new writers had by then stirred up a major controversy with their claims for widespread innovations in literature. Yet Hugo's gradual conversion to the cause of French Romanticism during the 1820's lacked the manifest boldness of his pronouncements after the *Préface de Cromwell* in 1827. Until that time, he had been content to claim merely: "to wish to replace the outdated and false colors derived from pagan mythology with the new and fresh colors inspired by the truths of Christian theology." [27] Reassured by the praise and adulation that *Hernani* had won for him in 1830, as the most prestigious member of the new school, he engaged in the publication of a number of prefaces to his own poetry which he presented in the form of manifestoes. Despite the many embarrassingly naïve assumptions they contain, these prefaces serve as a fairly accurate record of the various dimensions that Hugo's own poetry had begun to assume after 1830.

If Hugo by comparison with Lamartine was cautious about articulating a social program for the Romantic poet, he displayed remarkable consistency in asserting the poet's social and political missions after 1830. The poet's commitment to his age must manifest itself by the testimony which his work gives to the struggle of men in their attempts at social definition.

And, let us mention it at least in passing: in this conflict of men, doctrines, and interests which fling themselves out at us so violently every day in the works produced by this century, the poet has a serious task to perform. Without going into his civilizing function here, it is for the poet to underscore political events as historical events when they merit such attention.[28]

The striking metaphors used by Hugo in his elaboration of the social responsibilities assumed by the Romantic poet attest to the strengthening of his convictions in these matters. From his descriptions of the poet as "the crystal soul" and the "resounding echo," Hugo is finally emboldened to define the complete poet in his preface to the volume, *Les Rayons et les Ombres* (*Beams of Light and Shadows*) in 1840: "The author believes that any true poet, regardless of his own beliefs, gotten from his arrangement of the ideas bequeathed him by eternal truth, must contain within himself the compendium of the ideas of his time." [29]

The assurance with which Hugo speaks of the poet's function in society reasserts itself more bluntly still in the poetry that follows the prefaces. Such statements merge so completely with his lyricism so as to constitute the central inspiration of the poems. The conception of the poet as guide, leader, educator and magus constitutes one of the major themes in the poetry of the social Romanticists. Such self-appointed advisers to the new society in need of direction and fulfillment receive their superior powers from the inspiration which God gives them.

> *Il rayonne! il jette sa flamme*
> *Sur l'éternelle vérité!*
> *Il la fait resplendir pour l'âme*
> *D'une merveilleuse clarté.*
> *Il inonde de sa lumière*
> *Ville et désert, Louvre et chaumière,*
> *Et les plaines et les hauteurs;*
> *A tous d'en haut il la dévoile;*

Car la poésie est l'étoile
Qui mène à Dieu rois et pasteurs! [30]

["He radiates! he casts his flame on eternal truth! He
makes it shine for the mind with a marvellous light.
With the light of his inspiration, he inundates cities
and desert, the Louvre and thatched cottages, plains
and plateaus; to everyone he unveils the light from up
high; for poetry is the star that leads kings and shep-
herds to God."] For Hugo, then, not only is the inspiration of the poet something divine, but so too is the
mission with which he has been entrusted. Both, the
message imparted in the poem and the kind of language in which it is conveyed, combine to define what
we consider to be the romantic elements in Hugo's
poetry. The use of such ready opposites or antitheses
as: cities and desert, palaces and peasant cottages,
plains and plateaus, reveals the expression of an individual who either enjoys the simple reassurances of a
child or who believes himself in possession of the kind
of knowledge which transcends common human experience. Hugo conceives the poet's function to be one
of mediation between man and God. The religious
dimension so evident in "Fonction du poète" is drawn
from what the poet feels to be his inspiration and it
remains inextricably intertwined with it. The personal
and intimate character of its expression is in perfect
accord with the kind of individualism defined by
Hugo as a requisite for Romanticism. In tone and
spirit, the religiosity of Hugo complemented the unorthodox zeal and inspiration that characterized the attempts at religious reform by such self-appointed
popes as Lamennais, Lacordaire, and Montalembert.
In a sense, Romanticism so conceived fits Ludovic
Vitet's cogent definition of 1825: ". . . Protestantism
in art and literature." [31]

Whatever lack of dialectical coherence may be discernible in Hugo's variously stated pronouncements
concerning the poet and his function, such statements

are nevertheless always endowed with the stamp of powerful conviction. After 1843, his conception of the poet is further complicated by an abnormal bereavement over the accidental death of his daughter, Léopoldine, and his subsequent exile on the islands of Jersey and Guernsey during the 1850's and 1860's. The bitterness he experienced in his banishment from France induced him to advocate a rejection of all semblance of order and leadership in Louis-Napoleon's Second Empire. Once again, the assurance of tone in which he speaks is of greater importance than the ideas which he expresses.

> *Pourquoi donc faites-vous des prêtres*
> *Quand vous en avez parmi vous?*
> *Les esprits conducteurs des êtres*
> *Portent un signe sombre et doux.*
> *Nous naissons tous ce que nous sommes.*
> *Dieu de ses mains sacre des hommes*
> *Dans les ténèbres des berceaux;*
> *Son effrayant doigt invisible*
> *Ecrit sous leur crâne la bible*
> *Des arbres, des monts et des eaux.*
>
> . . . .
> *Ces hommes, ce sont les poètes . . .*[32]

["Why, then, do you continue to ordain priests when you already have some among you? The leaders of humanity are marked by a dark and mild sign on them. We are all born that which we are. With his hand, God consecrates men in the shadow of the cradles; his frightening, invisible finger writes in their mind the gospel of the trees, the mountains, and the waters. These men, they are the poets of today."]

The flirtation with occultism during his exile in Jersey prompted Hugo to inject yet another dimension to the kind of spirituality that constituted the major theme of the sixth book of his collection, *Les Contemplations.* There is nothing in Hugo's verses to remind us of the orthodoxy of inspiration that frequently found its way into the writings of the more religiously-bent writers of the seventeenth and the eighteenth centuries. The kind of religion described in such poems as "Ce que dit la Bouche d'ombre" ("What the Mouth of Darkness Says") is obviously a profoundly Romantic religion since it is founded in the mystical belief in a world which participates in the being of God in a universal harmony. After 1856, such beliefs merge with Hugo's conception of the poet and his function:

> Imaginais-tu donc l'univers autrement?
> Non, tout est une voix et tout est un parfum;
> Tout dit dans l'infini quelque chose à quelqu'un;
> Une pensée emplit le tumulte superbe.[33]

["Did you imagine the universe any differently? No. There is but one voice and one perfume. In God everything says something to someone. There is but a single idea, and it permeates the superb hubbub of creation."] The Romantic style of a poet like Hugo must be discerned, then, by the method of expression which reveals the motives behind whichever ideas may be contained in the poems concerned.

If the social Romanticism of such poets as Hugo and Lamartine is to a large extent defined by the religious and pantheistic elements in evidence, Vigny's commitment to society is distinguished by its conspicuous absence of any positive theological allusions. The coherence with which Vigny developed his conception of the function of poetry has induced most literary critics and scholars to consider him the philosopher of the French Romanticists. Vigny's ultimate optimism is couched in the initial pessimism doubtlessly derived from the bitterness and disappointment he personally experienced. The poet, a superior but solitary figure, often the victim of the misunderstanding of the unappreciative society which he serves, stoically fights to preserve and further the cause of humanity through enlightenment. In Vigny's estimation, the message imparted by the poet for the benefit of future generations becomes ultimately divorced from the poet who generously bequeaths his ideas to mankind without expecting its immediate gratitude.

> *Le vrai Dieu, le Dieu fort, est le Dieu des idées.*
> *Sur nos fronts où le germe est jeté par le sort,*
> *Répandons le savoir en fécondes ondées;*
> *Puis, recueillant le fruit tel que de l'âme il sort,*
> *Tout empreint du parfum des saintes solitudes,*
> *Jetons l'oeuvre à la mer, la mer des multitudes:*
> *—Dieu la prendra du doigt pour la conduire au port.*[34]

["The real God, the strong God is the God of ideas. On our foreheads upon which fate has sown its seed, let us spread knowledge in productive waves; then, gathering the fruit such as it emerges from the mind that produces it, completely imbued with the perfume of the thinker's holy solitude, let us throw the work into the sea, the sea of the multitude: God with a finger will take it up and lead it safely to the shore."] Like his counterparts, Hugo and Lamartine, Vigny's conception of the social humanitarianism of the poet is deeply rooted in his own personal reaction to human experience. This personal ingredient in his poetry, however camouflaged at times, constitutes the identifying mark of his Romanticism.

It would be erroneous to assume that all of the French Romanticists accepted the call and commitment to social action. As early as 1832, Théophile Gautier protested what he considered to be the enslavement of art to the cause of pragmatism, claiming that such practical concerns were diametrically opposed to the notion of the beautiful, the only acceptable aim of real art. Bolstered perhaps by Hugo's somewhat anti-pragmatic statements as he declared them in his preface to *Les Orientales* in 1829, Gautier issued the following definition of all the fine arts: "Art is freedom, luxury, efflorescence; the blossoming of the soul in idleness." [35] If Gautier's anti-utilitarian conception of literature won the support of such Romanti-

cists as Petrus Borel, it remained a minority position
during the July Monarchy until the fall of the Second
Republic in 1851. Later dubbed as the writers of art
for art's sake, Gautier and Borel divorced themselves
from the mainstream of Romanticism in its period of
effervescence during the 1830's and 1840's. Without
directly advocating any special regard for the position
taken by Gautier in literary matters, Alfred de Musset
described his conception of literature in terms that
closely resembled the aims and methods of the poets
of art for art's sake. Identifying intensity of sentiment
and emotion with creativity, Musset asserted that ex-
cess and overindulgence were justified by the creation
of poems that could be taken for works of art. In an
effort to enlist the Romanticists to the cause of social
progress, Hugo issued the following interpretation of
art in 1864: "Be useful! Serve some cause. Do not
assume the pose of the disgusted when it is a question
of being efficacious and good. Art for art's sake may
produce beautiful works, but art in the service of progress is more beautiful still." [36]

The campaign by the leading French Romanticists
for a social utopia ended cruelly and abruptly in 1851
with the assumption of Napoleon III to power as
emperor. Any hope of continuing to press for social
and political amelioration was quickly extinguished by
the censorship imposed upon the writers. For the social Romanticists whose art was so intertwined with
social preachment, there remained the choice of withdrawal from the literary scene or exile. While the
majority of the writers chose the former solution, Romanticists such as Victor Hugo and Pierre Leroux
preferred banishment from France so that they could
continue to wage their campaigns for progress. After
1851, the way was clear for the fuller development of
the literary philosophy of art for art's sake because of
this adamant refusal to associate literature with social
issues.

Any serious attempt to arrive at a definition of

French Romanticism must take into consideration the historical contexts in which it was placed. More than merely a reaction to the controlled restrictions of Classicism and neo-Classicism, French Romanticism emerged at the beginning of the century as a conspiration with the spirit of the French Revolution in order to achieve greater freedom for literary expression. With the ensuing Industrial Revolution's absorption into the mainstream of French life, the equilibrium associated with the Old Regime had been definitively destroyed and the search for a new and more acceptable balance was initiated. Most of the writers who had hitherto concentrated on self-expression in prose and poetry soon became associated with the cause of fashioning a new and a more perfect France. Rejecting the view so popular with the eighteenth-century *philosophes* that man's unity could be achieved through a careful and balanced use of reason, the Romanticists sought to append the more personal *mystiques* of emotion, sentiment, and intuition to reason in order to arrive at a more comprehensive view of the universe. What the Romanticists attempted to do was to propose the total aggregation of man's conscious and subconscious powers to the cognitive process. By their admission of the complexity of human experience, these writers of the nineteenth century ushered in the age of Modernism which has continued to our time. French Romanticism, then, emerges as something more than a preponderance of ideas and views; it represents the initiation of a mode of expression and an attitude toward life that retains a measure of validity today. Baudelaire's definition of its accomplishment states the case most succinctly: "Romanticism does not rest precisely in the choice of subject matter nor in the particular truth that it may impart; rather, it rests in the manner of expressing human feeling." [37]

2

Alphonse de Lamartine
and the Neo-Classical Inheritance

The enthusiastic reception accorded the collection of
twenty-four poems [1] known as the *Méditations poétiques* (*Poetic Meditations*) in 1820, constitutes the
most telling revelation on the nature of Lamartine's
early lyricism. The freshness of inspiration and the
delicately-sustained elegiac tone elicited the enthusiasm of the advocates of change and the defenders of
traditionalism alike. The younger readers reacted posi-
tively to the undeniable sincerity of expression so
manifest in the poetry, while their conservative counterparts were reassured by the poet's unmistakable allegiance to neo-classical forms and techniques. Whatever literary innovations may have been contained in
the poems of 1820, they were not immediately apparent at least to those readers who were anxious to
recognize some adherence to the accepted methodology. The themes of love, anguish, despair, melancholy,
and death in the *Méditations poétiques* could scarcely
be regarded as revolutionary in French poetry, and the
frequent appearances of worn metaphors, periphrases,
biblical terms, and mythological allusions were devices
that pointed rather to the direction of eighteenth-century strophic lyricism. Yet the spontaneity of emotion
and sentiment joined in an effusive and melodious
language heartened the young readers of 1820 who
had been so avidly seeking out the articulation of their
own feelings and experiences in literature. The ironic
fact of the matter was that Lamartine's collection of

poems owed no debt to either the neo-Classicists or the Romanticists. The poet avoided any scrupulous observance of neo-Classical techniques for fear that they would distort his sense of personal urgency. Nor could the young Romanticists speak convincingly of Lamartine's purported allegiance to their cause in 1820. Whatever remnants of classical method or hints at romantic innovation may have been discernible in Lamartine's early verse, they were more likely the result of the poet's unconscious adaptation of the most prevalent writing styles or his personal reaction to certain life experiences.

The feeling of sadness and resignation that dominates the *Méditations poétiques* constitutes their central theme and motif. Each poem evolves from the poet's direct confrontation with some experience; his search for peace and contentment has led him away from the society of men to the bosom of a seemingly more sympathetic and benevolent nature. The love lyrics are inspired by Lamartine's early love for two women: Graziella, a teen-aged Neapolitan whom he knew during a trip to Italy in 1811, and the matronly Julie Charles with whom he had become acquainted in the summer of 1816. Although the poems celebrating Lamartine's feelings for Graziella are among the most frequently ignored in the collection, such poems as "L'Adieu" ("The Farewell") and "Le Golfe de Baïa" are filled with the same kind of spontaneous sincerity and feeling of melancholia that characterizes the poems of the so-called Julie cycle. Lamartine's adroitness at transposition of his experiences into his poems probably accounts for the degree of pleasure with which they provided neo-classical traditionalists and radical innovators. There can be no mistaking Lamartine's intense lyricism in such poems as "Le Lac" ("The Lake") and "L'Isolement" ("The Isolation"), for example, despite the fact that such lyricism is often camouflaged by the use of language that is both discreet and objective. The inspiration of such poems, however rooted in Lamartine's love episode with Madame Charles at the Lake Bourget, transfigures the personal experience in order to suggest more directly man's destiny and human predicament. Lamartine purposely refrains from any specific mention of Graziella and Julie Charles by name; they are referred to simply as "Elle" ("She") and "Elvire," an obvious idealization of woman. The conspicuous absence of any appreciable amount of concrete detail contributes in giving the majority of the poems in the *Méditations poétiques* their somewhat abstract and universalized effect. Lamartine's apt generalizations and transfigurations of his particular love experiences enable the reader to identify more directly with the sentiments and the emotions expressed. Thus, the poems often achieve the level of individual meditations on human destiny while retaining their basic lyrical qualities.

By so ably transforming his love experiences into tragic idylls, Lamartine succeeded in joining his own problems to the more general problems confronting man. The use of vague, ethereal, and semi-abstract language in most of the *Méditations poétiques* strips the poems of their suggestiveness and permits them to emerge as idealized love lyrics of purity and innocence. The poems in the "Julie cycle," for instance, are effective evocations of the ill-starred lover whose sorrow has become transfigured by the recollection of a time gone-by. With the adroit aid of his memory and imagination, Lamartine has managed to recreate his experience with Julie with an appropriate amount of personal intensity. In thus pleading with nature to safeguard the memory of his transitory moments of happiness, the poet invites the reader to meditate on man's fate by underscoring the pain and anguish that he now experiences. But it is principally the poet's intensely experienced anguish such as is expressed in the poems that causes their transformation into meditations on human destiny without their loss of any lyrical quality. The essentially lyrical tone that pervades the meditations accounts for their being considered romantic innovations.

The spirit of sadness that pervades the love poems in recollection of Graziella and Madame Charles provides a logical springboard for the more philosophical and religious verse that concludes the *Méditations poétiques*. Yet in his melancholy, Lamartine points to the harmony that exists between nature and the feelings of man. Nature plays the role of comforter to man, reflecting as it does for the poet the grandeur of God through its own beauties. The contemplation of nature leads the poet to make an eventual declaration of faith, which in turn allows him to experience a sense of peaceful resignation to life. Whatever doubt the poet may have entertained concerning the seeming indifference of a haughty nature proves to be momentary, and the majority of the poems end with a note of exhaltation and hope. The state of a bittersweet melancholy and a quiet resignation to his plight as a man marks the poet's ultimate fulfillment in the *Méditations poétiques*. Despite a heavy insistence upon imagery that conveys a sense of loss and near-despair in such poems as "L'Isolement," "Le Vallon" ("The Dale"), and "L'Automne" ("The Autumn"), for instance, the closing stanzas always carry forth constructive statements on human life. Whatever uncertainty may betray certain verses of the love poems, such concluding poems as "L'Homme" ("Man"), "Le Désespoir" ("Despair"), "La Foi" ("Faith"), and "L'Immortalité" ("Immortality") counteract such an impression with their blunt and moral assertions on the existence of an afterlife. Yet even these exhortations for man to resign himself to the will of God emerge more as a personal appeal than as overbearing moral preachments. The reader cannot help but remember the personal anguish in the poet's words and recall his sense of personal loss even in these somewhat more pretentious poems. Thus, despite the sadness that permeates the *Méditations poétiques*, they are the poet's personal affirmation of hope and faith.

Despite their outward conventional appearance, these lyrics represented an important stage in the development of French lyricism. Whatever awkwardness in neo-classical technique remained was more than counterbalanced by the overall songfulness of the poems themselves. To understand the effect these poems had on the readers of 1820 requires perhaps a temporary abandonment of our twentieth-century critical sense. Whatever else, Lamartine's verse was a marriage of words with mood and emotion that constituted the kind of language unseen and unheard in France since the sixteenth century. To the readers of the *Méditations poétiques* in the early 1820's, what mattered most was the unadorned directness of communication achieved in the majority of the poems. The predictable yet delightfully musical strain of Lamartine's verse spoke an intuitive language that made itself understood to the readers without the usual recourse to the humdrum conventions of a complex exterior world. The union of the poet's feelings and emotions with nature scenes succeeded in conveying the poet's uncertainties with such intense urgency to an audience largely in sympathy with such a mood and such an attitude. The greatest single virtue of the *Méditations poétiques* resides in their ability to suggest a twofold vision: the first one emanating from the private world of the poet, and the second one projecting from the recognizable world of everyday realities. The total effect of the poems is one of intimacy and sincerity; the messages conveyed are only second in importance to the manner in which they are conveyed.

Lamartine's sublimation of his love experience with Madame Charles in "Le Lac" serves as an excellent example of the poet's effective communication of his emotions with such directness:

> Ainsi, toujours poussés vers de nouveaux rivages,
> Dans la nuit éternelle emportés sans retour,
> Ne pourrons-nous jamais sur l'océan des âges
>   Jeter l'ancre un seul jour?

O lac! l'année à peine a fini sa carrière,
Et près des flots chéris qu'elle devait revoir,
Regarde! je viens seul m'asseoir sur cette pierre
  Où tu la vis s'asseoir!

["Thus, always thrust forth towards new shores, car-
ried forever into the unending night, will we ever be
able to cast anchor upon the ocean of time for a single
day? Oh lake! the year has scarcely run out, and near
these beloved waves that she was scheduled to see
again, look! I come alone to sit upon this stone where
you saw her sit down!"] Lamartine's opening quatrains appropriately make use of a maritime term in its
most primitive sense to evoke the passage of time.[2]
The poet recalls his love for Madame Charles as he
revisits the scene of their meeting the previous summer. The seemingly prosaic expression, "ainsi," plays a
double function in this evocation: the word conveys
the poignant crystallization of the moment of realization that such a store of thoughts and emotions has
been accumulated in the secret recesses of the soul.
Too, when read and heard in its relationship to the
twice repeated "ainsi" of the third stanza, it is utilized
as an anaphora to stress the melancholy that has overtaken the poet in his return to the lake. The old and
visibly outworn metaphor, "l'océan des âges," to signify simple time is perhaps the image that most of-
fends contemporary critics. Yet it is undeniable that
this metaphor links the ideas of time fleeting by; it
blends neatly into the manner in which Lamartine has
chosen to present his major theme. The reference to
Madame Charles as "elle" in the second line of the
second quatrain may well be the poet's intention to
avoid indiscretion in the neo-classical tradition, yet
such discretion, in this instance, constitutes better art
since the pronoun "elle" records faithfully by its very
allusiveness the silent language of the mind. The harmony achieved between the scene described and the
emotions conveyed gives the poem its stamp of genuine lyricism. The personification of the lake in the

second quatrain enables it to signify and symbolize human nature in general since it becomes witness to the loves of all men. Thus, the individual reader is able to identify with the poet's predicament because it is presented as a reflection of the human predicament.

Lamartine's lyrical sense does not always achieve the sense of balance and restraint throughout the *Méditations poétiques*. The relatively general and semi-abstract terms employed in such a poem as "Le Lac," for example, enable the poem to obtain its quasi-objective effect despite its discernible lyric quality. The so-called romantic or personal elements in such a pessimistically-inspired poem as "L'Isolement" upsets the kind of balance obtained in "Le Lac." Written several months after Madame Charles' death in 1817, "L'Isolement" bespeaks the poet's inability to attain any kind of consolation in this world. Only the thought of rejoining his beloved in the afterlife prevents the poet from despairing. Composed at his home in Milly, "L'Isolement" expresses Lamartine's attempt to regain his lost equilibrium. His picturesque description of nature betrays the wildness of his imagination in this particular instance more than a plausible respect for fact.

> Souvent sur la montagne, à l'ombre du vieux chêne,
> Au coucher du soleil, tristement je m'assieds;
> Je promène au hasard mes regards sur la plaine,
> Dont le tableau changeant se déroule à mes pieds
>
> Ici gronde le fleuve aux vagues écumantes;
> Il serpente, et s'enfonce en un lointain obscur;
> Là le lac immobile étend ses eaux dormantes
> Où l'étoile du soir se lève dans l'azur.
>
> Au sommet de ces monts couronnés de bois sombres,
> Le crépuscule encor jette un dernier rayon;
> Et le char vaporeux de la reine des ombres
> Monte, et blanchit déjà les bords de l'horizon.

["Frequently, on the mountain at sunset, I sit down, sadly, in the shadow of the old oak tree; haphazardly, my eyes survey the plain whose changing scene takes place at my feet. Down here, the river with its foamy waves rumbles, meandering and plunging itself into a far-off abyss; over there, the placid lake stretches its sleepy waters to where the evening star rises from the blue. At the summit of these mountains capped with dark trees, the twilight emits a last beam of light; and the moon rises and clouds the edges of the horizon."]

Lamartine's heavy reliance upon auditory and visual imagery in the first three quatrains of "L'Isolement" fails to give us any truly precise impression of the nature setting because of the vagueness of the sounds and the colors that are conveyed. Yet the imprecision of his nature descriptions convincingly sets the tone for the reverie that unfolds during the remainder of the poem. The reverie and not the landscape setting is what matters most to Lamartine in his poem. The poet displays a certain disregard for fact in "L'Isolement." We know, for example, that there are no such large expanses of land in the vicinity of Milly, such as the plain that is evoked in the first quatrain, and that the small streams that grace the region are hardly susceptible of producing the foamy waves that are alluded to in the second quatrain. Rather, the nature setting in "L'Isolement" finds its basis in the poet's dreamy melancholia and feeling of disenchantment.[3] Such descriptions of nature are endowed with much more subjectivity than we may first realize; whatever reality they may suggest is intrinsic to the poem itself. Yet the poet takes refuge in nature in order to convey his melancholic mood; its contemplation reminds him that he is in exile and eventually spurs him on to quest for the ideal. The intuitive rapport that the poet experiences with nature accounts for the rather volatile and evanescent quality that the background descriptions appear to possess. As an effective externalization of the poet's feelings and emotions, "L'Isolement" looms as an excellent example of what T. S. Eliot termed in 1919 as the *objective correlative*.

The readers of "L'Isolement" doubtlessly recognized in the poem the symptoms of the *mal du siècle* such as had been described earlier in Chateaubriand's *René*. Nearly all of the lines in the poem suggest in some way the disgust and disenchantment which the poet feels. The old oak tree in the first quatrain conveys the aloofness from everyday activity in that as a symbol of old age, it conjures up the lack of real life activity and dynamism. The poet chooses the twilight rather than the dawn to contemplate the scene, and such a casual phrase as "au hasard" intensifies the sentiment of futility experienced. He sits on the mountain watching the meandering river engulf itself into some dark abyss; the poet likens himself to the river that seems devoid of purpose and direction. The "lac immobile" of the second quatrain reinforces the sense of death and stagnation that overwhelms the writer. The slow, monotonous rhythm of the poem is marvellously suited to the subject of "L'Isolement." The poem, however, ends on a hopeful and almost exultant note: the poet in his contemplation of nature emerges with the conviction that happiness may exist perhaps in the afterlife. With this realization, the tone of the verses shifts from the quiet yet mournful sounds of resignation to the excited repetitive exclamations of hope and expectation.

> Là, je m'enivrerais à la source où j'aspire;
> Là, je retrouverais et l'espoir et l'amour,
> Et ce bien idéal que toute âme désire,
> Qui n'a pas de nom au terrestre séjour!

["There, I would intoxicate myself at the fountain to which I aspire; there, I would retrieve the hope and the love, and the ideal which every soul desires, and which remains indefinable on earth!"]

Despite the fact that Lamartine's imagery conveys a sense of vagueness and imprecision, the immediate overall effect of "L'Isolement" is one of clarity of thought. There can be no mistaking the mood that pervades the entire poem. The limpid verses are the result of the poet's direct outpouring of his intensely-felt emotions. The sentiment of loss and the expectation of some future happiness, although relegated to the past and the future, are almost dramatically intensified by the nature of the poet's subjective reaction to nature in the present. Lamartine's conscious awareness of both an exterior and an interior reality enables him to convey his personal impressions in the manner that made itself understood by both his traditionalists and romanticist readers.

Lamartine's popularity among both the traditionalist and the revolutionary factions during the 1820's may be partially explained by his somewhat transitional position between these two groups. His religious and political views, for instance, such as are discernible in his publications, strike us as moderately liberal ones for his time. Cautiously avoiding the extremism of such radical reformers as Lamennais and Pierre Leroux, Lamartine preferred to strive for more gradual changes within the established structure and order of the day. If the conservatives were attracted to him, it was perhaps because they saw in him a reliable advocate of moderation and the status quo. The fact was that his political philosophy appeared to an extent determined by his religious convictions. Outwardly, he always paid lip service to Catholicism. Yet his religious position may be only described as an unorthodox one; it rejected the principle of revelation and consequently a majority of the Church's dogmas. Politically, Lamartine took a dim view of the association of Catholicism and the Crown, and he shared Lamennais' view that the whole of Christianity was in urgent need of reform through a critical re-examination of the spirit of the New Testament. However uncomfortable he may have felt in the Church, Lamartine avoided any outward break with it, a fact that no doubt reassured his more conservative audience. For the more discerning readers, however, his poetic expression betrayed his participation with other Romanticists in a movement to redefine and recast accepted theological conceptions to make them fit the needs of the time. Such modernization, of course, entailed the kind of doctrinal transformations that stripped religious belief of its orthodoxy and caused it to reflect, rather, the personal views and interpretations of the authors in question. Most of Lamartine's poetry reflected such a tendency.

The second collection of poems (1823), *Nouvelles Méditations poétiques* (*New Poetic Meditations*), did not meet with the same popular success enjoyed by Lamartine's earlier volume. Although the general tenor of the poems translates the poet's happier mood —such poems as "Ischia" and the "Chant d'amour" ("Song of Love"), for example, echo the joyous experience of living—the lingering yet admittedly faded memory of Julie Charles prompts Lamartine to render her one last homage with his poem, "Le Crucifix." Largely inspired by the sight of the crucifix that Madame Charles was alleged to have clutched and embraced with her dying lips, "Le Crucifix" contains large draughts of the type of religious sentimentality that eventually became associated with Romanticism. The crucifix described by the poet is one almost completely divested of its traditional symbolism, so closely identified is it with the personal reactions of its beholder.

> *Et moi, debout, saisi d'une terreur secrète,*
> *Je n'osais m'approcher de ce reste adoré,*
> *Comme si du trépas la majesté muette*
>   *L'eût déjà consacré.*

> *Je n'osais! . . . Mais le prêtre entendit mon silence,*
> *Et, de ses doigts glacés prenant le crucifix:*
> *'Voilà le souvenir, et voilà l'espérance:*
>   *Emportez-les, mon fils!'*
>
> *.   .   .   .   .*
>
> *O dernier confident de l'âme qui s'envole,*

Viens, reste sur mon coeur! parle encore, et dis-moi
Ce qu'elle te disait quand sa faible parole
        N'arrivait plus qu'à toi . . .

["And I, standing, overwhelmed by a secret terror, did
not dare approach these beloved remains; it was as if
at the moment of her death, her body was consecrated
by the silent majesty. I did not dare! . . . But the
priest understood my silence, and from her icy fingers
he removed the crucifix: 'There is the souvenir and the
hope that remains, my son, take it with you.' . . . Oh!
you, the last confidant of the soul that flies to you;
come, closer to my heart, and speak; tell me what she
was telling you when her weakened voice finally only
reached your ears . . ."]

The emotional impact that the very sight of this
particular crucifix produces in the poet[4] very nearly
divests the object of its usual symbolism, although the
poem does preserve an essentially religious strain.
What is of particular interest, however, is the manner
in which the poet arrives at his consideration of the
crucifix as the symbol of man's life in death. Lamartine's conclusions are dictated directly by the grief
that the sight of the object engenders in him. The
crucifix is given to him with the expectation that it
will inspire him with hope. But the poet's hope is
generated more by the knowledge that his beloved
professed belief in the power of the crucifix that she
kissed before dying. The poet's first reaction upon
receiving the cross that last touched his beloved's lips
is to ask the revelation of her final thoughts. The faith
of the poet, such as it expresses itself in "Le Crucifix,"
seems rooted at once in the belief of an afterlife and in
the assurance that such a woman must share in eternity. His affirmation of belief is ultimately linked to
the emotions and the sentiments provoked in him by
the crucifix in question. The intuitive assurance that
he feels causes him to assert his creed in so presonal-
ized a manner.

The peace and serenity which Lamartine enjoyed

during his long stay in Italy in 1827 inspired the codification of his personal and religious philosophy in the
collection of poems published in 1830 under the title,
Harmonies poétiques et religieuses (*Poetic and Religious Harmonies*). By and large, the poems are a fusion of the poet's lingering sense of melancholia produced by vivid reminders of death with an almost
overstated expression of confidence in the existence of
an afterlife. The harmony which the poet sees and
hears is the wordless hymn that emerges from the
beauties of the whole of creation in praise of God the
maker. Like Chateaubriand before him, Lamartine
conceives the unity of outer and inner reality in terms
that are purely emotional and aesthetic.[5] The
pantheism frequently suggested in such poems as
"Hymne du matin" ("Morning Hymn") and "Jéhovah ou l'idée de Dieu" ("Jehovah or the Idea of
God") betrays an appeal that is perhaps more poetic
than religious. Lamartine's vision of God emanates
more from his feelings than from his conviction in the
poem, "Jéhovah:"

> *Montez sur ces hauteurs d'où les fleuves descendent,*
> *Et dont les mers d'azur baignent les pieds dorés,*
> *A l'heure où les rayons sur leurs pentes s'étendent,*
> *Comme un filet trempé ruisselant sur les prés.*
>
> . . . .
>
> *Quand la terre, exhalant son âme balsamique,*
> *De son parfum vital enivrera vos sens,*
> *Et que l'insecte même, entonnant son cantique,*
> *Bourdonnera d'amour sur les bourgeons naissants;*
>
> *Quand vos regards noyés dans la vague atmosphère,*
> *Ainsi que le dauphin dans son azur natal,*
> *Flotteront incertains entre l'onde et la terre,*
> *Et des cieux de saphir et des mers de cristal,*
>
> *Ecoutez dans vos sens, écoutez dans votre âme,*
> *Et dans le pur rayon qui d'en haut vous a lui:*
> *Et dites si le nom de cet hymne proclame*
> *N'est pas aussi vivant, aussi divin que lui!*

["Climb to the heights from where the streams trickle
down and whose golden feet are bathed by the azure
skies when the rays of light stretch out over the slopes
like wet streaks dripping down into the meadows. . . .
When the earth emits its embalmed smells, your
senses will become intoxicated by its perfume, and
even the insect, humming its hymn, will buzz with
love around the flowering buds; when your vision is
drowned in the hazy horizon, like the dolphin in his
own blue waters, floating in uncertainty between the
waves and the land, and the sapphire sky and the
crystal seas, listen to your senses, listen to your soul,
and in the pure rays of light that shine on you, [and]
tell me if the name which that hymn proclaims is not
as alive and as divine as the hymn of nature!"]

The *Recueillements poétiques* (*Poetic Contemplations*) of 1839 mark the poet's evolution from the almost exclusively elegiac and lyrical strains of his earlier
collections to the adoption of a more visible attitude
of social humanitarianism. Lamartine's social and political preoccupations, destined to articulate themselves by his candidacy for election to the presidency
of the Second Republic in 1848, were in part motivated by the profound sense of grief that overwhelmed
him when his only daughter, Julia, died during a trip
to the Holy Land in 1832. Despite a diplomatic career
begun in 1825 and such manifestations of his political
involvement as in the "Ode contre la peine de mort"
("Ode against Capital Punishment") of 1830, and in
the famous "Ode sur les Révolutions" ("Ode concerning Revolutions") of 1831 which announced his
evolved liberalism, Lamartine appears to have waited
until 1833 to enter the political arena with any real
sense of dedication. Henceforth, both his writings and
his political career underscore his greatest personal
mission: the enlightenment and emancipation of the
masses.[6] The inspiration and the intuition that characterized his more personally effusive poetry up until
this time give way to the social preachments made

after 1834. Lamartine publicly renounced the "narrow selfishness" that motivated his earlier verse in a poem written in 1839 and included in the *Harmonies poétiques et religieuses*, the dedication: "A. M. Félix Guillemardet." The personal strain that dominates the social Romanticism of Lamartine is perhaps best conveyed by the author himself in the poem to Guillemardet which he meant as a kind of manifesto. The two strophes that follow record both his evolution as a poet and the nature of his newly-acquired social sense.

> *Puis mon coeur, insensible à ses propres misères,*
> *S'est élargi plus tard aux douleurs de mes frères;*
> *Tous leurs maux ont coulé dans le lac de mes pleurs,*
> *Et, comme un grand linceul que la pitié déroule,*
> *L'âme d'un seul, ouverte aux plaintes de la foule,*
>   *A gémi toutes les douleurs . . .*
>
> *Alors j'ai bien compris par quel divin mystère*
> *Un seul coeur incarnait tous les maux de la terre,*
> *Et comment, d'une croix jusqu'à l'éternité,*
> *Du cri Golgotha la tristesse infinie*
> *Avait pu contenir seule assez d'agonie*
>   *Pour exprimer l'humanité!*

["Then, my heart was insensitive to its own misery; later, out of compassion it streched out in response to the sufferings of my fellow man; all of his pain was mingled with my tears, and like a great shroud unfolded by pity, a single soul was made sensitive to the complaining of the people, and it uttered a deep groan for all their pain . . . Then, I understood very clearly the divine mystery by which a single heart could embody all the hurt of mankind, and how the single cry from the cross at Golgotha, reaching into eternity, had been able to contain the agony sufficient to express the anguish of humanity!"] Lamartine's blending of social preachment with mysticism constituted the main fabric of most of his later attempts at educating the masses and found its ready complement in the pronouncements of the Saint-Simonians and the religious reformers of the time.

The epic, as a poetic form, unquestionably exerted a strong appeal to the majority of the French Romanticists. The ambitious challenge of the epic, its purported claims to narrate the beginnings and the destinies of the national and the universal human character, held a particular attraction for the most articulate social Romanticists who conceived of themselves as the responsible directors of the French conscience. The complex structure of the epic form, with its leisurely pace and its allowance for elaborate developments, provided just the kind of opportunity desired by poets who had ambitious humanitarian messages to impart. The two fragments of Lamartine's unfinished epic, *Les Visions*, were conceived as early as 1823 as a long series of related narratives and "epochs" meant to evoke the efforts of the human mind throughout the centuries to achieve its highest and noblest destiny. The philosophy underlying the idea of *Les Visions* is perhaps more revealing of the poet's Romanticism than the two fragments published in partial realization of the epic. Like Victor Hugo, Lamartine begins with an intuitive reassurance that his interpretation of the history of mankind embraces the most comprehensive view. His conviction stems from his own emotions and sentiments—his personal response to internal and external reality. The published fragments of *Les Visions* constitute a variegated blend of narratives, philosophical discourses, parables, idyllic, and elegiac poems. Despite their respective publication dates, *Jocelyn* in 1836, and *La Chute d'un ange* (*The Fall of an Angel*) in 1838, *La Chute d'un ange* was initially meant to precede *Jocelyn*, which Lamartine intended to serve as a conclusion to *Les Visions*. Jocelyn's abnegation and renunciation would redeem the fallen angel, Cédar, from his sin.[7]

Published under the full title, *Jocelyn, Journal trouvé chez un curé de village* (*Jocelyn, A Journal Found in the Library of a Village Priest*), the ten thousand lines that make up this fragment contain a prologue followed by nine epochs and an epilogue.[8]

Aimed at popular consumption, *Jocelyn* is the novel-ized account of the life of the *abbé* Dumont whom Lamartine had known during his youth. The altruistic Jocelyn chooses to study for the priesthood so that his sister may inherit the entire family fortune. The Ter-ror of the French Revolution, however, forces him to flee the seminary and to take refuge in the French Alps where he gives shelter to the orphaned daughter of a man hunted down by revolutionary fanatics. Joce-lyn falls innocently in love with his ward, Laurence, but dismisses any thought of marriage because of the strange request made of him by his imprisoned bishop. So that he may be administered the last rites of the Church, the bishop requires that Jocelyn give up any idea of marrying Laurence and consent to be ordained a priest in prison. Jocelyn thus gives up his love for the young girl in order to obey the condemned bishop. While ministering to the needs of the people in the mountain hamlet of Valneige, Jocelyn is called upon to administer the last rites to an unknown woman who turns out to be his beloved Laurence. He himself dies in an epidemic that ravages the entire mountain area.

Despite its unusual length, *Jocelyn* maintains its essential unity; everything in the prologue, the nine epochs and the epilogue centers around Jocelyn, the principal hero of the fragment. The secondary epi-sodes and moral developments are attached to the central story. Lamartine's theme or thesis is spelled out in unmistakably clear terms: the necessity of sacri-fice, suffering, and abnegation to achieve one's spirit-ual destiny. *Jocelyn* symbolizes by his attitudes the struggle which the individual soul can expect to en-counter in the quest for God. The social thesis discern-ible in *Jocelyn* is clearly subordinated to the spiritual theme that pervades the entire epic. The poet's ro-mantic temperament dominates most of the fragment; its most glaring manifestations account for whatever implausibility mars the reading of *Jocelyn*. Lamar-tine's narration frequently betrays a somewhat blunt disregard for fact and external reality. The bishop, for instance, displays a blatant ignorance of Catholic theology and tradition. Jocelyn himself exhibits a curious aloofness as the village priest supposedly concerned with the spiritual administration of his flock. Yet despite such inaccuracies and blemishes in portraiture, the fragment is illuminated by the touching lyricism that graces a significant number of pages. The ninth epoch of *Jocelyn*, by far the most satisfying portion of the fragment, contains the touching episode of "Les Laboureurs" ("The Tillers") in which Lamartine unfolds his social doctrine. It has been suggested that the entire section bears a striking resemblance in inspiration to the two paintings by Millet, *The Reaper* and *The Sower*.[9] The poet issues an appeal for wider appreciation of the simple and good life as led by the French peasantry, and betrays his personal nostalgia for the ancestral land. Lamartine's celebration of country life captures the bucolic scene with particular vividness at times. Yet the characters that inhabit his idyllic poetry are almost completely divested of any real sense of individuality; they emerge more as symbolic representations of the ideal peasant type than real people. Such romantic symbolization fitted neatly into the pattern of Lamartine's humanitarian vision; [10] he reveals a tendency to relegate his characters and his nature settings into the background in order to spell out his moral and social messages.

C'est l'Angélus qui tinte et rappelle en tout lieu
Que le matin des jours et le soir sont à Dieu.
À ce pieux appel le laboureur s'arrête,
Il se tourne au clocher, il découvre sa tête,
Joint ses robustes mains d'où tombe l'aiguillon,
Elève un peu son âme au-dessus du sillon,
Tandis que les enfants, à genoux sur la terre,
Joignent leurs petits doigts dans les mains de leur mère.

["The bell tolls the Angelus and reminds everyone everywhere that their days and nights are a gift of God. At this pious sound, the tiller stops and turns towards the belfry; he removes his cap, clasps his two strong hands from which the goad falls, elevates his thoughts a bit above the furrows, while the children, kneeling on the ground, join their little fingers with their mother's hands."]

The simplicity and the lyrical tenor so much in evidence in *Jocelyn* was doubtlessly responsible for the enthusiastic reception which it received in 1836. Despite an annoying desultoriness in presentation, certain glaring syntactical errors, and inconsistencies of style, Lamartine's fragment bespoke the breath of inspiration which elicited the kind of emotional response that he wished from his readers. The general success enjoyed by such publications as *Jocelyn* bore eloquent testimony to the type of literary evolution that had overtaken France since the Revolution of 1789.

La Chute d'un ange, originally intended as the initial episode of the unfinished *Visions*, is divided into fifteen "visions," all of which center upon the eighth vision which formulates Lamartine's poetic and philosophical creed.[11] Lamartine's epic about the fallen angel, Cédar, prior to the great flood recalls Lord Byron's similar concern with the plight of angels in his mystery drama, *Heaven and Earth*. The Romanticists' obsession with the acquisition of an all-encompassing knowledge and vision excited their fascination for angels such as Lucifer who had been punished for their pride and presumption. For poets such as Lamartine and Hugo, convinced of the authentic voice behind their inspiration and eager to think of themselves as reflections of the divine, the position of the fallen angel piqued both their imagination and their curiosity. Such a preoccupation predicted the eventual identification of such angels with the myth of Prometheus for Hugo in the sixth book of his *Contemplations*.

The angel, Cédar, falls in love with the mortal Daï-dha who had been entrusted to his care, and is con-

demned to live in human exile. Persecuted by Daï-
dha's tribesmen in Lebanon, captured by the giants of
Babel and betrayed by the guide who was to have led
Cédar, Daïdha and their two children into Mesopota-
mia, the man-angel is finally committed to the desert
where his children die of thirst and Daïdha goes mad.
Immediately preceding the first drops of rain of the
great Deluge, Cédar commits suicide by throwing
himself on the burning funeral pyre that was meant to
consume his family. *La Chute d'un ange* underscores
the plight of primitive man not yet endowed with the
moral sense of human suffering. The theme of revolt
against suffering is often conveyed with striking effect
thanks to Lamartine's dramatic imagination. Whatever talent Lamartine may have demonstrated in *La
Chute d'un ange* as an adept psychologist in the more
dramatic and epic portions, the fragment failed to win
the approval of readers and critics alike. The ambitious conception of *La Chute d'un ange* was overshadowed by its partial and unsatisfactory realization.

The most accessible of the French Romantic poets
during the 1830's and 1840's, Lamartine's verse from
the *Méditations poétiques* to the lengthy "La Vigne et
la maison" ("The House and the Vineyard") bears
the stamp of spontaneity and directness of expression.
Most of his poems display his dexterity in manipulat-
ing the imagination to speak so unassumingly to the
emotions of his readers. The seemingly effortless ease
with which he managed to crystallize his personal
inspiration in poetry with a simplicity of form that
appealed to all types of readers accounted for his influence and popularity among traditionalists and innovators alike. His publications betray the kind of cautious
evolution from social and political moderation to liberalism that was susceptible of enlisting the support of
both factions at once. Lamartine's poetic and political
expression stemmed directly from his personal and

emotional response to experience. His ability to adapt and adjust his form and his ideas to the shifting moods of a difficult era explains why his writing gave the impression of being dictated by a lingering sense of neo-Classicism and a vibrant conception of Romanticism.

3

Alfred de Vigny,
Preacher in an Ivory Tower

The outer reserve or discretion that characterizes the
poetry of Alfred de Vigny stands in sharp contrast to
the more facile and effusive lyricism of such notable
counterparts as Lamartine, Hugo, and Musset. A
heavy reliance upon epic, dramatic, and narrative devices strips Vigny's verse of the type of directness of
expression and confessional tone that are so readily
identifiable in the work of most French Romanticists.
A conscious artist and technician, Vigny sought out
the philosophical implications in his personal experience before transposing it into his poetry. Many of his
poems unveil the effort of quiet and painstaking
discernment; some poems may strike us, at first, as
impersonal and generalized reflections on the human
predicament. If Vigny is usually referred to as the
"philosopher" of Romantic poetry, it is more in recognition of the coherence of his doctrine than for any
real profundity of thought. To a great extent, Vigny
went to considerable lengths to camouflage his personal ideas and emotions in his poetry. Indeed, his
poems are little more than the symbolic manifestations
of his ideas. Recurrent use is made of symbols in order
to endow his thought with a sense of concreteness of
expression and of dramatic form. Yet the symbols
utilized by Vigny contain the clue to his identity as a
Romantic poet. As concretizations of his ideas, the
symbols resorted to in the collections, *Poèmes antiques
et modernes* (*Old and Modern Poems*) and *Les Desti-*

nées (*The Fates*), do not always suggest easy and ready identifications with the ideas that are expressed. The poet's distortion of such symbols as Christ in "Le Mont des Oliviers" ("The Mount of Olives") and Moses in "Moïse," for example, reveals his need to force the symbols to conform to his own conception. An examination of Vigny's symbols demonstrates that, by and large, they serve as paper-thin disguises for the poet himself. The figures of Moses and Christ are made to reflect so completely the ideas and attitudes of Vigny that they are ultimately divested of their traditional symbolic significance and are instead assimilated by the poet's personality.

The cautious yet firm optimism that the poet voiced in the posthumously-published *Les Destinées* (1864) [1] was, to a degree, fashioned from the pessimistic stance of his earlier years. His pessimism was rooted in his own interpretation of history and in his observations of reality; it asserted itself with quasi-aphoristic force, somewhat reminiscent of Pascal, in an 1835 entry into *Le Journal d'un poète* (*The Diary of a Poet*): "It is certain that the work of Creation has been badly botched; at best, it remains half-done: it evolves so slowly and painfully toward perfection." [2] An unhappy childhood and adolescence, disappointments in love and marriage, unsuccessful military and political careers—all served to corroborate whatever pessimistic views he may have evolved from his early readings and experiences. It cannot be denied that his poetical works do translate his disenchantment with life: his principal themes underscore man's inexorable fate and destiny, the treachery of women, the indifference of God and nature and the abject loneliness which the poet or the superior man experiences. Yet as early as 1823, Vigny reveals in his poem, "Le Déluge" ("The Flood"), a certain oscillation between doubt and faith in God and man that ultimately resulted in the mitigated optimism decreed in his last and most important collection, *Les Destinées*. The expression of confidence arrived at in *Les Destinées* is inspired by his constructive stoicism or resignation to his fate. Bequeathed Voltaire's practical philosophy of human progress, Vigny preaches from a distance on the necessity of man's adjustment to his condition: we must act as if we hoped. Eschewing the enthusiasm and the sweeping generalizations of his more hopeful counterparts, he stands as an advocate of limited action and social change. The poet's function, he tells us in "La Maison du berger" ("The Shepherd's Hut"), is to discern for the people between those acts whose accomplishment is susceptible of improving man's lot, and the futile acts and gestures that not only needlessly expend energy but impede progress and enlightenment. Vigny's conception of a human brotherhood stems in part from his systematic rejection of any theoretical or metaphysical explanation of the human condition. Confronted by a silent God and an indifferent nature, man must learn to grope courageously and stoically toward his own betterment. Therein lies the potential greatness of man in Vigny's estimation. His religion is the religion of ideas that preaches a limited faith in human progress. The priests and guides of such a religion—the poets—must entrust their fame and appreciation to posterity.

The *Poèmes antiques et modernes* of 1826 comprise twenty-one poems which are divided, according to inspiration, into three groups: the mystical poems, the ancient poems, and the modern poems. The first group contains such notable pieces as "Moïse," "Le Déluge," and "Eloa ou la soeur des anges" ("Eloa or Sister to the Angels"), all of which assert Vigny's growing sense of pessimism through his adaptation of biblical figures as symbols of modern man's predicament. The Book of Antiquity includes the poem, "La Fille de Jephté" ("Jephthah's Daughter"), which translates Vigny's protest against unjust chastisement, but the greater number of poems in the Homeric cycle are little more than pale adaptations of André Chénier's pagan poems of the preceding century. The unevenness of the Modern Poems is somewhat offset by the memorable "Le Cor" ("The Horn"), a successful reverie evoking the heroic medieval legend of Roland and Charlemagne at the pass of Roncevaux in the Pyrenees. In all, the four or five distinguished poems contained in the *Poèmes antiques et modernes* point to the generally significant verse of *Les Destinées*.

Written in 1822 and inserted into the so-called "mystical" cycle of the *Poèmes antiques et modernes*, "Moïse" remains Vigny's most elaborate pronouncement on the function and position of the nineteenth-century Romantic poet. Vigny's retreat in 1838 to the "ivory tower" in Charente is clearly predicted in this remarkable poem of his early career. As he himself so readily acknowledged, the Moses of the *Poèmes antiques et modernes* is not precisely the Moses of the Old Testament; he is rather the poet's convenient symbol of the genius or the superior man. "Moïse" assumes a somewhat dramatic structure; it may be conveniently divided into the following three categories: prologue, monologue, and epilogue. The first part, the prologue, skillfully alludes to the weariness of the aging prophet as he contemplates in isolation the nearby Promised Land from an incline that also surveys the small groups of Jews assembled in anticipation. Moses knows that he will not enter into the Promised Land and meditates upon the meaning of his life. In the monologue or attempted dialogue with God, Moses lists the miracles which he has accomplished through God as his prophet. He complains bitterly about the abject loneliness of his state as leader of the Jews; he is respected but not loved, he has not found happiness but has grown powerful in his isolation from his fellow men. The third part or the epilogue conveys God's response to Moses: it is implicit in Joshua's election to succeed the dying Moses, the prophet's work will be appreciated and acknowledged only by posterity. The parallelism between the prophet and the poet is the major theme elicited in "Moïse." Like the prophet, the poet is elected by God to share in his comprehensive vision of creation. Just as the prophet's special powers are derived from an inner force—his collaboration with God, so too are the poet's vision and articulateness derived from the inner forces of an inspiration that is not always corroborated by exterior reality. The prophet-poet, however, must pay an awful price for his special powers: his superiority denies him membership in the fraternity of men.[3]

> *Hélas! vous m'avez fait sage parmi les sages!*
> *Mon doigt du peuple errant a guidé les passages.*
> *J'ai fait pleuvoir le feu sur la tête des rois;*
> *L'avenir à genoux adorera mes lois;*
> *Des tombes des humains j'ouvre la plus antique,*
> *La mort trouve à ma voix une voix prophétique,*
> *Je suis très grand, mes pieds sont sur les nations,*
> *Ma main fait et défait les générations.—*
> *Hélas! je suis, Seigneur, puissant et solitaire,*
> *Laissez-moi m'endormir du sommeil de la terre!*

["Alas! you have made me wise among the wise! My direction has guided a wandering people to safety. I have caused fire to descend upon the heads of kings; kneeling, posterity will adore the laws that I have brought down; I open the most ancient of human tombs, and death finds in my voice prophetic words. I am very great: nations are at my feet, I have fashioned and unmade whole generations with my hands. Alas! Lord, I am powerful yet alone. Allow me to sleep the sleep of the earth!"]

Like the type of Romantic hero later to be evolved by Vigny in such poems as "La Mort du loup" ("The Death of the Wolf") and "La Maison du berger," the Moses of the *Poèmes antiques et modernes* is a stoical Moses, willing to accept the responsibilities of such an attitude. He is conscious that his position and the nature of his mission alienate him from the people he wishes to help; they are unable to understand and appreciate the enormity of his sacrifice in their behalf. Vigny's Moses offers psychological resistance to the accomplishment of the will of God; consequently, he is made to appear more human than the Moses of the Old Testament. As a kind of allegory of the genius and the superior man, the Moses described in the poem emerges as a Romantic character so readily identifiable with the poet himself.

In "Le Déluge" (1823), Vigny asserts his metaphysical pessimism basing himself upon a biblical episode to underscore the tragic undertones of man's predicament. Doubtlessly influenced by Byron's *Heaven and Earth* and perhaps inspired by Poussin's *The Flood*,[4] the poem sheds light upon the motives behind Vigny's later refusal to complicate his notion of social humanitarianism with any theological or metaphysical considerations. "Le Déluge" bespeaks the poet's defiant expression of protest against the kind of God who would so indifferently punish the innocent and the just along with the wicked. The poem's conclusion is punctuated with religious skepticism; at the very least, it states the poet's waivering between doubt and faith. The lengthy narrative centers around the lamentable plight of Emmanuel and Sarah who are condemned to drown with the wicked because of their mutual desire to be with each other. Vigny manipulates biblical material in such a way so as to make it conform to the particular theme that he wishes to project. The last line, for example, betrays a distortion of the Old Testament account. The biblical reference to the rainbow at the end of the deluge was meant to symbolize God's reconciliation with man; Vigny's transposition of the account underscores his cynical view of the matter.

Ce fut le dernier cri du dernier des humains.
Longtemps, sur l'eau croissante élevant ses deux mains,
Il soutenait Sara par les flots poursuivie;
Mais quand il eut perdu sa force avec la vie,

Par le ciel et la mer le monde fut rempli,
Et l'arc-en-ciel brilla, tout étant accompli.

["It was the last cry of the last human being alive. For a long time, with his two hands, he kept Sarah, pursued by the waves, afloat in the rising waters. But when his strength left him with his life, the world was filled with the sky and the sea, and the whole objective having been realized, the rainbow shone forth."]

The manifest individualism exhibited by the leading French Romantic poets in their handling of seemingly familiar religious topics prompts us to refer to such poetry more as religiosity than as religious verse. In their ambition to restore the spiritual dimension that had been neglected by the leading exponents of the Enlightenment, such poets turned to the study of the Old and New Testaments for fresh insight and inspiration. Dismissing the more orthodox interpretations of Christianity, for instance, they set out to re-examine scriptural accounts in the light of the modern problems that beset nineteenth-century France. The so-called religious poetry of the leading Romanticists strikes us as little more than awkwardly camouflaged projections of their own social, political, and humanitarian visions within the apparent framework of traditional religious themes.[5] The truth of the matter is that biblical figures appear recast and remade to fit more neatly into the molds that reflect the principal issues confronting the poets in question. Ironically, such poems reveal a conspicuous absence of any traditional religious feeling even though they may owe their inspiration to some obvious religious tenet. The individual inspiration of each poet causes him to seek out his own interpretation of Christianity; traditional religious belief is largely considered to be mythical, and the poet aims at transforming such myths into symbols more meaningful for a modern society. By so

divesting religious symbols of their traditional connotations of belief, the Romanticists secularized religious
meaning while still retaining its familiar exterior trappings. Such a de-christianizing process is widely evident in the works of Romantic painters and composers
as well as in such men of letters as Vigny and Hugo.
More so than the latter, perhaps, Vigny's personal
attitude toward Christianity evolved to the point
where he found it necessary to eliminate it entirely
from his doctrine of human progress and enlightenment.

The poem, "Le Mont des Oliviers," demonstrates a
greater indebtedness to the poet's own inspiration and
to such secularized conceptions of Christ as found
in the paintings of Mantegna (1431–1506) and
Proud'hon (1809–65) than to the scriptural accounts
of Matthew, Mark, Luke, and John. Vigny's Christ of
the Mount of Olives emerges as a strikingly vivid incarnation of the poet himself with his sense of frustration and helplessness. Although written in 1843 and
first published in the 1 June 1844 issue of the *Revue
des Deux Mondes*, "Le Mont des Oliviers" was inserted by both the poet and the editor, Louis Ratis-
bonne, in the major collection of philosophical poems,
Les Destinées,[6] published only after the poet's death
in 1864. Vigny's intention is made explicit in the section ending the poem, "Le Silence." The calm and
almost emotionless language of the final admonition
strikes out against traditional belief in Divine Providence. Vigny's implied thesis is singularly reminiscent
of the conclusion in Voltaire's *Candide*: man is meant
to live in metaphysical anguish; he must rather try to
work out his own destiny, courageously and stoically,
by his advocacy of human progress and fellowship
with men.

> *S'il est vrai qu'au Jardin sacré des Ecritures,*
> *Le Fils de l'Homme ait dit ce qu'on voit rapporté;*
> *Muet, aveugle et sourd au cri des créatures,*

Si le Ciel nous laissa comme un monde avorté,
Le juste opposera le dédain à l'absence,
Et ne répondra plus que par un froid silence
Au silence éternel de la Divinité.

["If it is true that in the sacred Garden of Scripture, the Son of Man said all that which we see recorded there; if Heaven remains silent, blind and deaf to the pleas of men, then it abandoned us like an aborted world. The just will oppose such indifference with disdain and will only answer, henceforth, with a cold silence the eternal silence of God."]

Vigny's "Le Mont des Oliviers" provides us with an excellent example of the type of Romantic religiosity that found its way into the works of many of the leading artists, composers, and poets of the time. The poem underscores the dramatic confrontation between humanity and the implacable will of God. Unlike the Christ of the New Testament, Vigny's Christ is incapable of resigning himself to divine decree. He has evolved into an essentially more humanized Messiah; he implores God the Father to endow humanity with the happy certitude and the confident hope necessary for the endurance of pain and suffering. In "Le Mont des Oliviers," Christ's entreaties to his father go unanswered: "the evening sky remains dark, and God does not reply." Vigny's Christ leaves the world in sadness, knowing that he has failed to accomplish his primary mission: to rid humanity of its doubt and anguish. The poet's Romanticism is fused with the religious pessimism that is so discernible. "Le Mont des Oliviers" is first of all Vigny's own interpretation of the mission and message of Christ. The poet has transformed the Christ of Scripture into the type of social humanitarian that asserted himself in the France of the 1830's and 1840's. The poem emphasizes his humanity more than his claim to divinity; rather than the son of God, he is the son of Man who suffers and commiserates with humanity and seeks to

better man's plight through the abolition of violence.
By his frequently effective use of melodramatic devices—such as the startling antitheses between the
white of hope and the black of despair—Vigny has
succeeded in unifying the events of the biblical account with the theme that he meant to convey.

The tendency to reinterpret the symbolism of
Christianity in purely modern and humanistic terms
may be traced to the secularized rendering of the artist
Proud'hon's *The Crucifixion* of 1822.[2] Proud'hon's
Christ resembles more the young man of the Renaissance, handsome and beardless, rather than the picture of the lacerated Christ depicted in such scenes
throughout the ages. Vigny's Christ in "Le Mont des
Oliviers" is more in conformity with Proud'hon's conception than with the more traditional interpretation.
The Virgin Mary in Proud'hon's painting is likewise
portrayed in a purely humanistic manner; her suffering
and despair upon viewing her dead son has caused her
to faint at the foot of the cross. Vigny's emphasis on
the identification of death with despair in the first part
of "Le Mont des Oliviers" underscores the essential
humanity of his Christ. Searching the skies for a sign
of recognition from his Father, Vigny's Christ forsees
his impending death in terms that refer to human
grief by alluding to his mother as the widow.

> Mais un nuage en deuil s'étend comme le voile
> D'une veuve, et ses plis entourent le désert.

["But a black cloud of mourning unfolds like a widow's veil, whose pleats encompass the desert."]

In Vigny's estimation, it is evident that Christianity
has failed in its social and humanitarian mission.
However masked and restrained its language may appear, the second part of "Le Mont des Oliviers" points
an accusing finger at God for all the evil and injustice
in the world. Vigny's adroit manipulation of antithesis
between the terms that suggest hope and despair accounts for much of the poignancy of the section. The

increased use of words connoting despair anticipates the final message reserved for the last part of the poem. Man, with the departure of the Messiah that failed, is ultimately left to his own resources to achieve his destiny.

> Ainsi le divin Fils parlait au divin Père.
> Il se prosterne encore, il attend, il espère,
> Mais il renonce et dit: 'Que votre volonté
> Soit faite et non la mienne et pour l'éternité!'
> Une terreur profonde, une angoisse infinie
> Redoublent sa torture et sa lente agonie.
> Il regarde longtemps, longtemps cherche sans voir.
> Comme un marbre de deuil tout le ciel était noir;
> La Terre sans clartés, sans astre et sans aurore,
> Et sans clartés de l'âme ainsi qu'elle est encore,
> Frémissait.—Dans le bois il entendit des pas,
> Et puis il vit rôder la torche de Judas.

["Thus spoke the divine Son to the divine Father. He bows again, he waits, he hopes, but he gives up and he says: 'May your will be done and not mine, and for all eternity!' A deep terror, an infinite anguish increase his torture and his slow agony. He stares into the distance for a long time; for a long time he searches for something without seeing it. The whole sky was as sinister as a funeral marble; without the stars, without the dawn, and without the light of the mind, the earth shivered as it still does today. In the forest, he heard footsteps, and then he recognized Judas' torch on the prowl."] The short phrases that describe the despair of the world produce an almost rasping sound that endows much of the section with a certain dramatic intensity. When seen in its relationship to the rest of the poem, the third part completes the circle begun in the first section with its theme underscoring the silence of God. Both the tone and the content of "Le Mont des Oliviers" show the evolution undergone by the Romanticists in their handling of religious subjects. Whatever liberties in style and interpretation may be discernible in Lamartine's "Le Crucifix," for example, the kind of religiosity of sentiment prompted by the death of Madame Charles still retains a basic identification with traditional Christian belief. Vigny's "Le Mont des Oliviers" consciously avoids any such identification. The poet's negative attitude toward the effectiveness of religious institutions in meeting the needs of modern man explains his reluctance to share the enthusiasm of such writers as Lamartine, Lamennais, and Montalembert who hoped to refashion and modernize the social framework of Christianity.

Considered by some critics as the most important single poem in the collection, Les Destinées, "La Maison du berger," [8] when first published in the July 1844 issue of the Revue des Deux Mondes, was meant to serve as the prologue for a projected series of philosophical poems which failed to materialize. Probably inspired by Vigny's nostalgic souvenir of his mistress, Marie Dorval's country cottage, the poem impresses us as a cross between an imagined and real experience recorded from the vantage point of the poet's later years. On the surface, "La Maison du berger" may strike the reader as an inordinately long and confused piece whose principal themes seem more disjointed than linked together by any kind of unity. Roughly divided into six major sections, the poem is written in strophes of seven alexandrine lines each. The heaviness of form that results, including several notable instances of embarrassing awkwardness, conforms, in a sense, to the weightiness of the subject matter in "La Maison du berger." Indeed, most of the major themes developed in the eleven poems that constitute the posthumous collection of Les Destinées are touched upon in this long and somewhat rambling poem. The first part of "La Maison du berger" is an invitation extended to Eva, the poet's companion and a composite of the qualities of the ideal woman, to flee the city with him and seek out in nature the kind of "austere silence" conducive to reverie and meditation. The

tenth strophe suddenly bursts forth with a diatribe
against railroads, doubtlessly Vigny's personal reaction
to the tragic derailment at Versailles in 1842, that
continues with breathless pace until the twentieth
strophe. Then, Vigny begins a meditation on the function of poetry in a world grown more mechanized. His
fourth theme praises woman for the influence that she
exerts upon the poet and his poetry; her love for him
prevents him from growing insensitive to the needs of
his fellow man in the comfortable isolation of his
retreat in nature. The last two sections, comprising
Part Three, voice the poet's refusal to see in nature a
benevolent mother and reassert in exalted language
the love of man for woman. P.-G. Castex sees in "La
Maison du berger" the symbolic link between the central symbol of the poem and the itinerary of the two
lovers.[9] From the hut on wheels, the two lovers would
have journeyed to the New World ("La Sauvage"), to
the Orient ("La Colère de Samson" ["Samson's
Anger"]), and to the bramble of the Landes region
("La Mort du loup").

Despite Vigny's exalted praise of nature as the
source of reverie and meditation for man in a world
complicated by ugly and dangerous mechanization,
the final strophes of "La Maison du berger" underscore its indifference and its insensitivity to man. Nature offers man but temporary refuge from the distrac-
tion and turmoil of the city; the poet must delve
within himself to extract the resources that will assure
his well-being. Contrary to Lamartine who saw in nature a source of consolation for man, Vigny views
nature with distrust and caution. This feeling of alienation that nature produces in the poet found its first
expression in Madame de Staël's novel, Corinne
(1807), yet Vigny's stated opposition to it fits into his
program of intellectual and social progress. As P.
Flottes stated in his study of Vigny, it is rather the
philosopher than the poet who speaks in "La Maison
du berger."[10] The poem ends with a programmic note

for Eva, representing here mankind itself, with which the poet traces the stratagem that will enable human intelligence to vanquish the blindness and indifference of nature.

Mais toi, ne veux-tu pas, voyageuse indolente,
Rêver sur mon épaule, en y posant ton front?
Viens du paisible seuil de la maison roulante
Voir ceux qui sont passés et ceux qui passeront.
Tous les tableaux humains qu'un Esprit pur m'apporte
S'animeront pour toi quand, devant votre porte,
Les grands pays muets longuement s'étendront.

Nous marcherons ainsi, ne laissant que notre ombre
Sur cette terre ingrate où les morts ont passé;
Nous nous parlerons d'eux à l'heure où tout est sombre,
Où tu te plais à suivre un chemin effacé,
A rêver, appuyée aux branches incertaines,
Pleurant, comme Diane au bord de ses fontaines,
Ton amour taciturne, et toujours menacé.

["But as for you, do you not wish, my apathetic travelling companion, to dream while you rest your forehead on my shoulder? Come down from the peaceful threshold of the house on wheels and view those who have preceded us and those who will follow us. All of the human portraits inspired to me by a pure Spirit will become alive for you when, in front of our door, the large silent countryside will extend itself. Thus, we will walk, leaving but our shadows behind on this ungrateful earth where the dead have walked; we will speak to each other about them at the hour when all becomes darkened and when you like to follow the trace of some nearly obliterated path, in order to dream, leaning upon the unsteady branches, and crying like Diana at the edge of her fountains, for your uncommunicative love, and feeling always threatened."] On the philosophical level, "La Maison du berger" resists the establishment of the kind of association between nature and poet that is generally understood by Ruskin's conception of the pathetic fallacy.

Vigny's ultimate refusal to identify so closely with nature endows most of his lyricism with an appearance of aloofness or cold detachment that offers itself in sharp contrast to the more effusive nature poetry of Lamartine, Hugo, and Musset. For Vigny, nature does not supply the unifying principle that assures man of his desired equilibrium. Nature is revealed to be little more than the convenient receptacle wherein the poet is allowed to reflect and meditate in relative peace and isolation, and where he may attempt to solve the problems that prevent him from achieving self-definition.

As the symbolic portrait of stoical resignation, "La Mort du loup" ("The Death of the Wolf") [11] lays bare, once again, Vigny's habit of deliberately distorting fact and reality in order to make the imagery of his poems conform more readily to his interpretation of certain attitudes. The wolf in his poem, for example, possesses great dignity, beauty, and an urgent sense of purpose, qualities that are hardly associated with wolves in everyday contexts. Vigny reverses the usual order of supposition in "La Mort du loup:" instead of representing the enemy of man and civilization, man and civilization are represented as the enemies of the innocent and noble wolf. The hunting of the wolf, such as Vigny describes it, bears little resemblance to reality; the hunters are never directly seen except through the instruments of their murderous act. Any sense of irony that could have been achieved by so focusing the main theme on the wolf family is, to a large extent, cancelled by Vigny's frequent insistence upon details that are too pointedly realistic in a poem containing such philosophical pretentions. The *faire voir* realism of "La Mort du loup" detracts from the basic credibility of the theme because of the falseness of the situation. The exalted language of the conclusion (Part Three) provides a striking antithesis to the two preceding sections that relate the hunt and the death of the wolf in terms that wreak of heavy realism. While the vividness of these two sections contribute

undeniably to the elucidation of the final thesis, their
formal relationship to the third part produces such a
jarring effect as to destroy the unity of the poem.
Although not a souvenir poem in the manner of
Hugo's "Tristesse d'Olympio," ("Olympio's La-
ment"), Vigny's poem, in treatment of language and
in total emotional effect, bears a distinct kinship to it.
Both poems rely so heavily upon concrete details that
are pointedly realistic that they are unable to extract
any universalized response from the reader. "La Mort
du loup" is far from being the idealized expression of
the attitude of stoical resignation that is implied in
the last section.

Yet, for all the disparity of tone that exists between
the first two sections and the conclusion, Vigny never
resorts to sentimentalism in his description of the pit-
eous wolf that is hunted down by his nameless and
faceless hunters. To achieve the contrast between the
latter's great dignity and the former's baseness, the
poem reveals adept qualifications of certain realistic
details that effectively achieve the distinction between
the two. Such qualifiers as "big" and "powerful," for
instance, take on the meaning of grandeur and nobility because of their specific placement in the narration. Such notions, of course, are in keeping with the
ultimate conclusion of the poem, and, were it not for
the annoying shift in the manner of expression in the
last part, the overall effect of "La Mort du loup"
might have been more convincing. The idea of the
wolves' dignity proceeds directly out of the rhythm of
the sentences in the first section. The stances of the
animals are described in short phrases that are set off
in simple narrative form, in a sense, just as uncomplicated as the activity of the wolves.

> "Le père était debout, et plus loin contre un arbre,
> Sa louve reposait comme celle de marbre
> Qu'adoraient les Romains . . ."

["The father was standing, and farther away next to a
tree, his she-wolf was resting like the marble on

which the Romans used to adore . . ."] Vigny cuts away from the heavy realistic concreteness of his description, and presents the picture of the motionless stance of the wolves with almost classic simplicity. The wolves derive much of their dignity from the fact that they are accomplishing what is natural to their station in life. To enhance the sense of dignity of the she-wolf, Vigny concentrates on portraying her beauty; he likens her to a marble statue and alludes to the wolf that suckled the legendary founders of Rome, Remus and Romulus.

Stylistically, the whole poem unfolds in the form of a triangle with the setting, the *paysage*, representing the world as it appears to the poet: dark, gloomy, sinister, and filled with all types of traps and deceits. The wolf symbolizes the poet's noble reaction to this situation. Man, the hunter, represents the despicable, negative attitude of a thoughtless "civilization." The final conclusion that we are asked to accept is that the wolf's stance, in the poem, is more sensibly attuned to conditions as they really are. Thus, the wolf emerges as the easy personification of the kind of stoical resignation which Vigny has been suggesting throughout "La Mort du loup." The final admonition, stripped of any religious allusion, "To complain, to cry out, to pray—all are equally cowardly," fits more neatly into the secular program of intellectual progress implied in the title poem of *Les Destinées* than a poem like "Le Mont des Oliviers."

"La Flûte," first published in 1843 and included in Vigny's posthumous collection, is a reworking of the theme presented in "La Mort du loup," but this time within the more recognizable framework of the well-known myth of Sisyphus. Despite the working of the poet's imagination in this poem, the effect is largely one of a narration somewhat more objectively related. Vigny exalts the "courage of the fated man" who gains for himself a sense of dignity through the effort that he expends in the accomplishment of his seemingly futile tasks. Such men, of course, are readily identified with the mythological figure whose stoical attitude inspires in them expressions of pity and commiseration for their fellow men. In "La Flûte," Vigny equates idealism with the ultimate achievement of some more perfect afterlife, and the attendant limitations and failures of man with this life.

> Pour moi qui ne sais rien et vais du doute au rêve,
> Je crois qu'après la mort, quand l'union s'achève,
> L'âme retrouve alors la vue et la clarté,
> Et que, jugeant son oeuvre avec sérenité,
> Comprenant sans obstacle et s'expliquant sans peine,
> Comme ses soeurs du ciel elle est puissante et reine,
> Se mesure au vrai poids, connaît visiblement
> Que son souffle était faux par le faux instrument,
> N'était ni glorieux ni vil, n'étant pas libre;
> Que le corps seulement empêchait l'équilibre;
> Et, calme, elle reprend dans l'idéal bonheur,
> La sainte égalité des esprits du Seigneur.

["As for me who knows nothing and who shifts from doubt to dream, I believe that after death, when the union of body and soul will be achieved, that the soul will find again its clarity of vision, and that, judging its work with serene assurance, understanding completely and expressing itself easily, as powerfully and as queenly as its sisters in heaven, will weigh correctly and know visibly that its breath was uneven because of the faulty instrument, that its work was neither magnificent nor contemptible, not being free; that it was the body alone that prevented the attainment of an equilibrium; and that, in serenity, it takes up again in ideal happiness the holy equality of the spirit of the Lord."] "La Flûte" is more than a mere justification of Sisyphus; it is also a statement of the poet's sense of frustration when confronted by the inadequacy of his expression. The beggar's flute emerges as the personification of the written poem that is achieved in anxiety by the poet. Like the mendicant who kisses his flute so lovingly in the poem, the poet too comes to acknowledge his gift to communicate with his fellow man, however imperfect his talent may manifest itself in his work. The poor flutist knows that his crude instrument enables him to lighten the burden of mankind by transmitting his homely yet strangely soothing melodies, worthwhile approximations of his inner feelings. Likewise, the poet hopes that his verse will translate at least a measure of his inspiration. He recognizes in the word a conventional symbol that may succeed in linking outer reality with the silent language locked in the inner recesses of his soul.

"La Bouteille à la mer" (Bottle in the Sea") is a reinforcement of the two themes which Vigny had suggested in "La Flûte." Bearing the subtitle, "Counsel to an Unknown Young Man," the poem was initially written as the final piece in *Les Destinées*. The didactic intention of "La Bouteille à la mer" comes close to making it a program poem. In it, Vigny likens the position of the poet to that of the captain of a sinking vessel at sea; fated to die in the distressed ship, the seaman carefully records crucial information which he inserts into a small bottle that is flung into the sea in the hope that it will eventually be retrieved. Thus, his death is not in vain if future generations obtain and understand the ideas that he has bequeathed them. "La Bouteille à la mer" is Vigny's expression of hope and confidence for the future of mankind. The poet, like the sea captain, gives generously of himself to benefit posterity. The concerted efforts of poets and scientists will bring about the eventual reign of reason and enlightenment to the world. In a sense, the poem is an affirmation of the poet's faith in ideas as a benevolent force.

Vigny's belief in the progress and enlightenment of humanity through reason is patently buoyed by an intuitively-felt knowledge of the presence of a final benevolent Providence that accepts and encourages such efforts at the attainment of human perfection. It is the assurance behind the poet's asserted belief that distinguishes his message from that of his more ration-

alistic counterparts of the eighteenth century and that
imprints his verse with the indelible mark of inspiration and imagination that has become associated with
French Romanticism.

Intimately associated with Vigny's conception of
the poet misunderstood by the society which he serves
is the problem of the preservation of his poems, the
receptacles of the ideas that benefit humanity. If the
poem is destined to be understood and appreciated by
future generations, its form should be sufficiently
durable to survive the ravages of time. With Vigny
and Musset, the proper crystallization of poetic inspiration became a source of serious concern. Vigny's
symbolic equation of the poem with the glass bottle
that is thrown into the sea prefigures Baudelaire's
opaque perfume jar and Mallarmé's hermetically
sealed syntax. Vigny's bottle in the sea suggests, of
course, the evident antitheses of fragility and strength,
of the seeming minuteness of the jar in the immensity
of the ocean.

> Il lance la Bouteille à la mer, et salue
> Les jours de l'avenir qui pour lui sont venus.
>
> Il sourit en songeant que ce fragile verre
> Portera sa pensée et son nom jusqu'au port,
> Que d'une île inconnue il agrandit la terre,
> Qu'il marque un nouvel astre et le confie au sort,
> Que Dieu peut bien permettre à des eaux insensées
> De perdre des vaisseaux, mais non pas des pensées,
> Et qu'avec un flacon il a vaincu la mort.

["He [the captain] throws the Bottle into the sea, and
greets the future which, for him, has already arrived.
He smiles when he thinks that this fragile glass will
carry his thoughts and his name to some port, that he
enlarges the earth with some unknown island, that he
records a new star and entrusts it to destiny, that God
may allow destructive waters to sink ships, but does
not allow the destruction of thought, and that with a
bottle, he has triumphed over death."]

"L'Esprit pur" ("The Pure Spirit"), written some

six months before Vigny's death, may be considered as a legacy which the poet bequeaths to posterity. Addressed to Eva, the ten strophes of the poem define with pommeling thrusts his confidence in the forthcoming reign of mind over matter. "L'Esprit pur" also reaffirms Vigny's philosophical independence. If the opening poem of *Les Destinées* confirmed the pre-Christian interpretation of fate and destiny, the final poem of the collection, "L'Esprit pur" is a clear rejection of positivistic currents as the new force in man's life.[12] As Verdun Saulnier so adroitly interprets the message,[13] "L'Esprit pur" is Vigny's clever transposition of the religious significance of the dove of the Holy Spirit in Catholic dogma to the secularized victory of mind over matter as effected through the ideas of the enlightened poet. The religion of ideas alluded to in "La Bouteille à la mer" graduates to a level of personal mysticism in "L'Esprit pur." Vigny's God of ideas reveals himself in sharp antithesis to the kind of knowledge that is sensuous and concrete. Man's plight is centered in the realization that he is a combination of mind and matter; only through ideas that possess transcendence over matter can he eventually hope to end his enslavement to it. "L'Esprit pur" is in a sense, also, the reaffirmation of belief in the genius of the poet. To an extent at least, Vigny's initial pessimism concerning Creation as a work badly botched is reverted into an expression of quiet confidence and hope. Thus, the eleven poems that constitute the collection, *Les Destinées*, when seen in their relationship to one another, translate attitudes of cautious optimism. Vigny's poetry consciously shuns expressions of sweeping enthusiasm that characterize the verse of such social Romanticists as Lamartine and Hugo. Yet the mystical fervor that punctuates the messages of his counterparts finds its way into his work in more subtle and gentle doses.

Ton règne est arrivé, PUR ESPRIT, roi du monde!
Quand ton aile d'azur dans la nuit nous surprit,

Déesse de nos moeurs, la guerre vagabonde
Régnait sur nos aïeux. Aujourd'hui, c'est l'ECRIT,
L'ECRIT UNIVERSEL, parfois impérissable,
Que tu graves au marbre ou traînes sur le sable,
Colombe au bec d'airain! VISIBLE SAINT-ESPRIT!

["Your kingdom has come, PURE SPIRIT, king of the world! When your azure blue wing surprised us in the night, goddess of our principles, a roving war ruled over our ancestors. Today, it is the WRITTEN WORD, the UNIVERSAL WRITTEN WORD, at times imperishable, which you engrave in the marble or which you trace upon the sand, oh! dove with beak of bronze! VISIBLE HOLY SPIRIT!"]

The symbols to which Vigny reverts to convey his personal feelings in such collections as the *Poèmes antiques et modernes* and *Les Destinées* frequently produce a steadying and sobering effect on his lyricism. Pierre Moreau considers Vigny's symbolism as the result of his inner struggle to restrain and contain the urge to effusive self-expression for the sake of the messages that he wished to impart in his poetry.[14] The symbol, in fact, betrays his attempt to avoid the kind of embarrassing indiscretion concomitant with the confessional tone underlying the lyricism that is more exclusively personal. For Vigny, the symbol served as the convenient detour from such effusiveness. It provided the necessary junction between his inspiration and the philosophical attitudes that he insisted on conveying in his verse. At the same time, the symbol acted as a veil or a camouflage for whatever personal elements might have been present, allowing him to unfold his ideas with considerably more clarity and objectivity. As a covering agent for the principal theme, the symbol deters the reader from such evidence and prevents the poem from disintegrating into merely an emotionally impassioned plea. A close scrutiny of Vigny's poetry reveals his efforts to endow his inspiration and his thoughts with a poetic form and language that would ensure its survival against the ravages and prejudices of time and place. If the symbol to which he has recourse succeeds in masking the more obvious expressions of his personality, it does not purport to rescue the poem completely from its inherent subjectivity. The symbol merely allows the poem to convey its basic theme with more directness by relegating the subjective elements to the background. The poet's subjectivity is, in a sense, cushioned with the cloak of surface objectivity. What elements of Romanticism remain may be found within the symbol itself and behind its seemingly objectified representation. Yet Vigny's sustained utilization of symbols rescues his poetry from the type of effusiveness that frequently mars the verse of some of his well-known counterparts.

In the *Journal d'un poète*,[15] Vigny defines the creative process as a search for the point at which the meaningful experiences of life can be elevated in order to cross the path of thought. To project his ideas with the kind of forcefulness that he sought, Vigny selected fables that were generally both moving and evocative. The frequently subtle and effective handling of a wide variety of imagery complicated the symbolism of his poems with definite subjective colorations. His insistence upon qualifying certain images to convey such contrasting attitudes as hope and despair, good and evil, doubt and knowledge, for example, bequeaths to such concepts the intimacy of his poet's imagination and inspiration. Vigny relies considerably upon the evocative power of his images to impart the major themes of his poems. By juxtaposition and transposition of many of the auditory and visual images that he employs, he often manages to suggest varying shades and degrees of intensity in his settings. The mood and the tone that emerge from the poetry appear directly but unobtrusively linked to the imagery that is linked or interrelated with the symbolism. Despite the out-

ward form of the narrative that the great majority of
his poems possess, the *Poèmes antiques et modernes*
and *Les Destinées*, for the most part, shun the kind of
rhetorical enlargement or embellishment that characterizes some of the more typical Romantic verse in the
nineteenth century.

The two major sources of imagery that are found in
Vigny's poetry could conceivably have stamped it with
the mark of neo-Classicism. Yet Vigny eschews em-
ploying the images that he borrows from ancient mythology and Holy Scriptures in any traditional sense.
Such learned allusions are instead usually stripped of
their more orthodox connotations and are used principally to endow that which is common or prosaic in the
human predicament with the indelible stamp of dignity and authority. In "La Maison du berger," for
instance, the poet-thinker of postrevolutionary France
is likened to the Roman god, Terme, ruler of bounda-
ries and landmarks. The poem, "Les Oracles," equates
the modern political situation with the machinations
of the Egyptian pharoahs, while "La Colère de Samson" ("Samson's Anger") alludes directly to the
wrathful nature of the God of the Old Testament to
convey the passion for vengeance aroused in the poet
himself because of the treachery of a woman. Vigny
casually identifies his ancestors in "L'Esprit pur" with
Nimrod, the hunter, and refers to the personification
of Romantic poetry in "La Maison du berger" as the
daughter of Orpheus. The sustained courage of the
beggar in "La Flûte" is compared to the futile yet
admirable position of Sisyphus, and Noah's dove of
peace in "La Bouteille à la mer" is adroitly manipu-
lated so as to suggest the shift from traditional religious belief to the poet's more secular espousal of faith
in ideas.

With similar effectiveness, Vigny uses such obvious
imagery as the desert sands and the ocean's waters not
only to convey the idea of vastness and expansiveness
in his poetry, but more especially to suggest with poign-

ancy the situation of the poet in isolation. More intriguing, however, is the author's dual conception of fire imagery; it is described at times as a beneficial force and as a destructive element. In "La Maison du berger," for example, the railroad is equipped with the fiery teeth of destruction as it proceeds in its opposition to man and its eradication of the shepherd's hut. In another section of the same poem, however, fire serves to inflame the enthusiasm and ecstasy that enable the poet to produce his verses. The fact that Vigny is able to ascribe different levels of meaning to his imagery invites the view that, unlike such congeners as Hugo, he possessed no logical, comprehensive view of the world. As Frank P. Bowman has suggested,[16] Vigny's verse is to a degree "a beautified statement of partial truth." The negative aspect of fire is invoked in such poems as "La Colère de Samson" and "La Mort du loup," whereas its more constructive power is emphasized in "Les Oracles," for instance, where the flames succeed in snuffing out political intrigue. In "La Sauvage," fire is defined as the purifying agent through which civilization is implemented.

To convey the idea of servility—the great depths to which man has sunk in Vigny's estimation, the familiar imagery of the wild animal and of the beast of burden is employed to good effect in the eleven poems that constitute Les Destinées. Somewhat reminiscent of La Fontaine's animals in the Fables, Vigny's beasts also serve to delineate particular characteristics of humanity. It should be noted that animals appear only in the most pessimistic sections of poems. By so degrading the portrait of man to the animal level, much of the pessimism of Vigny's personal views announce themselves in an indelible fashion. The use of the image of beasts of burden suggests the inactivity and the passivity of men which the poet condemns in unmistakable terms. In the opening poem, "Les Destinées," for example, men are likened to flocks of sheep and oxen with heads bowed to the furrow. In

"Wanda," the Russian aristocrats are herded together like sheep in the Siberian prison. The image or metaphor of the wild animal is often equated with spirited and active individuals. Delilah in "La Colère de Samson" is compared to a supple leopard; in "La Maison du berger," Eva's mind leaps like a gazelle from one thought to another, and the train's speed is described as faster than the leaps and bounds of the stag. The plight of the Indian woman in "La Sauvage" is likened to that of a starving wild hound, and to depict the grim fate reserved for the family of Abel, Vigny resorts to the image of the starving wolves.

> *Et le chasseur Abel va, dans ses forêts vides,*
> *Voir errer et mourir ses familles livides,*
> *Comme des loups perdus qui se mordent entre eux*
> *Aveuglés par la rage, affamés, malheureux . . .*

["And Abel, the hunter, goes into the empty forests and sees his livid families wandering and dying, like desperate wolves that bite one another, blinded with rage, starving and wretched . . ."] The metaphor of the stoic wolf in "La Mort du loup" elicits perhaps the greatest single impact in *Les Destinées* despite the repugnance provoked by such an unpoetic image.

The auditory and visual imagery utilized by Vigny in his more philosophical poems convey the sense of the poet's personal identification with often surprising subtlety. The silence of isolation in "La Maison du berger" is contrasted with the streamlined, efficient silence of "progress," and the poem issues a moving description of the cries of an oppressed humanity heard above the calm and implacable silence of an indifferent nature. Vigny employs visual images, references to such colors as black and white and red, in those poems that treat of death. The colors, black and white, are used in antithesis to each other, a telling device exploited by most Romanticists who translate their thoughts and emotions into vivid, absolute, and categorical language. The black skies in "Le Mont des Oliviers" contrast with the white shroud to symbolize despair overwhelming the hope of Christ. If Vigny relies upon the use of black to suggest the complete desolation of man, such colors as green, gold, and azure blue are referred to in order to suggest optimism in the victory of reason and enlightenment over matter. For example, the golden warmth of the sun shines upon the bottle cast into the sea at the end of "La Bouteille à la mer" suggesting the survival of ideas. Significantly too, is Vigny's description of the azure gold and diamond-colored waves that attract the ship's attention to the bottle in the ocean.

By his craft as a poet as well as by the inspiration and the imagination that moves his pen to commit his ideas to paper, Vigny reveals himself as a discreet practitioner of the type of social Romanticism that swept France during the two decades that preceded the Revolution of 1848. Despite his reluctance to join with his more enthusiastic congeners in the vociferous campaigns for reforms, Vigny in the reassuring surroundings of his ivory tower in Charente preached the new religion of ideas that he hoped would wipe out disease and ignorance from the new France that sought the establishment of a more acceptable equilibrium.

Vigny chose the voluptuous beauty of poetry to crystallize his philosophy. He selected his imagery for its ability to convey and reinforce his thought and for its beauty, weaving metaphor, color, and symbol together to give expression to the Idea. The metaphors in his poetry, drawn from literature, from nature, and from living creatures, attain a level of highly evocative power. At times, his images may have too strong an effect, as in the case of the dying wolf. It is true that much in his verse lacks the delicacy of charm usually associated with less serious lyricism. Yet, there is great beauty to be found in such descriptive scenes as the desert in "La Colère de Samson" and the travel sequence in "La Maison du berger." The drama of the metaphorical situation of Vigny's Christ in "Le Mont des Oliviers" and that of Samson in "La Colère de Samson" captures the reader in the reality of its psychological study.

4

Victor Hugo and the Prophetic Vision

The widespread association still made today between the name of Victor Hugo and the term Romanticism attests to the prominence that he enjoyed within the movement both in France and on the Continent during the nineteenth century. The wide range of his poetry from the early academic declamations of "Les Vierges de Verdun" ("The Virgins of Verdun") to the cabalistic symbolism of the posthumously-published collections, *La Fin de Satan* (*The End of Satan*) and *Dieu* (*God*) recounts the history and the development of French Romanticism in the most tellingly comprehensive terms we have. The seventeen volumes of poems that were published during Hugo's long lifetime (1802–85) [1] and shortly after his death unfold both his evolution and that of French poetry from the neo-Classicism and the social Romanticism of the first part of the century to the school of Art for Art's sake and the Symbolism or Modernism of the last five decades. The entire gamut of Hugo's verse is rescued from the limitations of his thought and messages; the power of his imagination and the suggestiveness of his imagery are discernible traits that characterize a significant number of his poems in such widely divergent collections as *Odes et Ballades* (1826), *Les Orientales* (1829), *Les Voix intérieures* (*Inner Voices*) (1837), *Les Châtiments* (1853) and *Les Contemplations* (1856). The last two volumes of poetry and the unfinished epic, *La Légende des siècles*

(1859 and 1885) constitute Hugo's greatest legacy to the French Romantic movement and to the restoration of lyricism in France during the nineteenth century. Despite whatever embarrassing pretentiousness may have dictated the poet's intention in these collections, their undeniably convincing and moving lyrical strain overshadow such shortcomings and make their reading an enjoyable and worthwhile experience.

It has already been stated that the originality of French Romanticism rests much less on the idealism of its messages than on the manner in which such idealism is conceived and expressed. The whole history of western thought and civilization reveals the efforts of mankind to derive a meaningful sense of unity and balance from the confusion of a world that asserts itself in terms that are mostly fragmentary and heterogeneous. The evolution of social, political, and religious institutions from ancient times to the French Revolution records the various solutions attained by man in his attempts to explain the enigma of man in the universe. Such views were necessarily geared, in varying degrees, to the existing structure of the time, and whatever reforms were advocated were understandably defined and limited by such frames of reference. The French Revolution was a categorical rejection of the Old Order for its inability to provide and maintain an equilibrium that could meet the requirements of a society that had grown significantly more complex. In its dramatic rejection of the literary principles that guided and dictated French expression since the seventeenth century, Romanticism emerged as the literary corollary of the social and political revolution of 1789. Dismissing the purely rationalistic tenets of the Enlightenment as inadequate to shape modern thought, the French Romanticists sought the extension of expression through their recognition of the roles of instinct, intuition, and inspiration in the cognitive process. The appendage of such faculties to reason, they maintained, would permit man to attain knowledge that was more comprehensive. This view, somewhat cautiously and conditionally endorsed in the verse of Lamartine and Vigny, was destined to receive its fullest statement in the poetry of Victor Hugo. The study of the poet's slow progression to such an attitude constitutes a study of Hugo's verse from his beginnings in 1820 to the early 1840's which marked the turning point in his life and work.

The completed version of *Odes et Ballades* (1828) includes poems published earlier under various titles in 1822, 1824, and 1826. The collection of 1828 affords us the opportunity of examining the technical and intellectual development that took place in the poet's early career. The odes and ballads that constitute the final version of 1828 underscore Hugo's sustained political and religious conservatism even though they serve as a subtle delineation of his evolution from neo-Classicism to a moderately-stated acceptance of some of the innovations of Romanticism. Such obvious odes as the "Mort du duc de Berry" ("Death of the Duke of Berry") and "Naissance du duc de Bordeaux" ("Birth of the Duke of Bordeaux") bespeak the kind of official and circumstantial flavor that hardly qualifies them to be considered lyrical expressions. The nostalgic Bonapartist ode to heroic action in "Mon Enfance" (1823) ("My Childhood") is already a moderately effective personal statement of the *mal du siècle* experienced by the poet when he calls to mind the glory and excitement associated with the Imperial regime. The ode, "A M. Alphonse de L[amartine]" composed in October of 1825 strikes a revealing chord in the development of Hugo's poetics. Advising Lamartine that he must ignore the criticism and lack of understanding of the "epicureans" that prefer to read voluptuous verse, he goes on to define the nature of true lyric poetry:

> *Telle est la majesté de tes concerts suprêmes,*
> *Que tu sembles savoir comment les anges mêmes*

Sur des harpes du ciel laissent errer leurs doigts!
On dirait que Dieu même, inspirant ton audace,
Parfois dans le désert t'apparaît face à face,
Et qu'il te parle avec la voix!

["Such is the majesty of your supreme concerts, that
you seem to know even how the angels manipulate
their fingers on the harps of heaven! One would think
that even God, the inspiration of your boldness, appears to you from time to time in the desert, and that
he speaks to you with the voice that is manifest in
your verse!"]

Whatever else, *Les Orientales* liberated French versification of its restrictive use of vocabulary and of the
stiffness of its metrical system. Aside from a group of
poems inspired by the Greek War for Independence,
most of the verse in the collection is impregnated
more with a sense of the picturesque than with any
profoundly personal emotion. As the newly recognized
leader of the Romanticists, Hugo asserts himself as the
spokesman for the repressed victims of the Greek Revolution in such poems as "Têtes du serail" ("Heads in
the Harem") and "Mazeppa" and "L'Enfant grec"
("The Greek Child"), no doubt influenced by
Eugène Delacroix's *The Massacres of Scio*, painted in
1824. The orientalism of Hugo is, in fact, his imaginative description of the Spain that he had visited during
his youth while his father, the General Hugo, was
stationed near Madrid. Complicated by his later readings and his interest in the Near East, the Orient
depicted in *Les Orientales* is one imbued with fantasy.
Whatever falseness may be discernible in his interpretation of the East is to a large degree compensated by
the vividness and suggestiveness of his imagery. The
mosques, gardens, and steps that he describes are conveyed in such picturesque language that we are ready
to ignore their essentially Spanish flavor.

The Preface to *Les Orientales*, in the tracks of the
explosive *Préface de Cromwell* of 1827, proclaims the
freedom and gratuity of art in terms that predicted the

later pronouncements of Théophile Gautier, the chief exponent of art for art's sake during the 1830's: [2] "Let the poet go where he wishes, doing what he likes; that is the only rule. The poet is free." Such statements mark his evolution from literary conservatism to the expansiveness and freedom of Romanticism. With characteristic verve for masking fact and testimony in order to make his point with more *éclat* than precision, Hugo bemoans the lack of greatness in French literature in the following terms: "Other nations say: Homer, Dante, Shakespeare. We say: Boileau."

Les Orientales reveal Hugo's unmistakable mastery of French versification. Indeed, the most sustained single impression that is conveyed to the reader is the poet's masterful handling of the formal elements that constitute the collection. The poem, "Les Djinns," for instance, contains seven different types of metre that ascend and then descend from the climax that is achieved in precisely the eighth strophe. The "Djinns" for Hugo represent the evil spirits of the night as they approach with terrifying intensity and gradually disappear in the distant calm. The poem is little more than a technical *tour de force*. As with so many poems that make up *Les Orientales*, the idea in the poem seems to weave itself gradually into the imagery. In other words, the inspiration or the basic idea emerges as an obvious extension of the principal images. The cadences and the increasing and decreasing sonorities produced in "Les Djinns" remind us, to an extent, of the effect that is achieved in Ravel's *Bolero*. Like the *Bolero*, also, "Les Djinns" is more attractive and pleasing for its novelty than for the theme that it actually unfolds. Yet, the poem does betray Hugo's unfailing sense of instinct; the dramatic form of "Les Djinns" does blend neatly with the sense of fright and terror that he meant to portray. The imagery of the poem, the haunting crescendoes and decrescendoes contribute to the kind of purely external musical effects of this minor verbal symphony. [3]

The mournful strain detectable in some of the verse

of *Les Voix intérieures* (1837) is a projection of the
kind of poignancy which Hugo's poetry will achieve
with sustained force during his years of exile on the
islands of Jersey and Guernsey. The death of the last
Bourbon king, Charles X, the admitted infidelity of
his wife with Sainte-Beuve, the passing of his brother,
Eugène,[4] all served to unnerve the poet and to increase
his already noticeable sense of insecurity to the point
where he felt compelled to voice his almost paranoiac
complaint in a poem addressed to his *alter ego*, "A
Olympio." For the most part, the lyricism of *Les Voix
intérieures* is somber. Yet such rêverie discernible in
"La Vache," for instance, announces the kind of attitude toward nature which the poet comes to adopt in
"Tristesse d'Olympio" of the collection, *Les Rayons et
les Ombres*. The last volume of poems to appear before his exile, *Les Rayons et les Ombres* (1840) reveals Hugo's slow evolution toward an increasing acceptance of the creeds and aesthetic codes of the
French Romanticists. Somewhat more imbued with
the social humanitarianism of his noted counterparts,
the overall effect of the collection is more purely lyrical than it is utilitarian. Among the best-known love
poems of Hugo, and of all French poetry for that
matter, is "Tristesse d'Olympio" ("Olympio's La-
ment"), composed in 1837 and inserted into the volume of 1840. Written with his mistress, Juliette
Drouet, in mind, "Tristesse d'Olympio" is an evocation of the places where Hugo had spent many happy
moments in the valley southwest of the city of Paris.
His return to the property of the Bertin family pro-
vokes a meditation upon the passage of time that is
underscored with sadness and regret. Yet the poem is
far from conveying a pessimistic message; in the face
of the seeming indifference of nature, Hugo expresses
faith in the power and durability of the human memory to conserve the fleeting moments of happiness
experienced by man. At the time of its composition in
1837, Hugo had not suffered the loss of his mistress;

the anguish of "Tristesse d'Olympio" is prompted by the realization that his love for her has become transformed with the passing of time. The external natural setting of the Bièvre valley, recently rejuvenated by the spring, serves as an annoying reminder to the poet that his experience is doomed to disappear into cruel anonymity in the great receptacle of nature.

"Tristesse d'Olympio" illustrates one of the most popular themes of French Romanticism: the attempt to achieve both an ideal and permanent expression of human love. The resultant anguish and agony suffered by the poet when he recognizes that his efforts meet with failure constitutes one of the major motifs of Romantic love poetry. Like Lamartine before him, Hugo expressly isolates his passion in nature, far from the crass considerations of a bustling and pragmatic world. Too, by so situating his love experience in a natural setting, he is more easily capable of conjuring up an association of purity and innocence, thus succeeding in appealing to a greater majority of his readers for sympathy. If Lamartine resolved the problem of the disconcerting transitoriness of human experience through the transfiguration of his love for Madame Charles, Hugo attempts to solve the problem by calling our attention to the more positive value to be found in remembrance and recollection. "Tristesse d'Olympio" is comprised of some thirty strophes, which may be divided into five parts, each of which may be considered as logical developments leading up to the resolution of the problem which Hugo presents. The first two strophes, serving as an introduction, reveal to us the slightly melancholic poet revisiting the scene of his love experience. These strophes constitute somewhat the reversal of the pathetic fallacy: nature does not reflect the sadness of the poet. The introductory strophes act, then, as a kind of prelude to the theme developed by the poem as a whole. The negatives of the first three lines are counteracted by the positive statements contained in the next nine lines which act as effective antitheses. The vague and general language of the introductory strophes conveys an almost religious atmosphere which is, to a degree, cancelled out by the documented inventory of realistic details which roughly comprise the make-up of strophes three through seven and constitute the second part of "Tristesse d'Olympio." The elaborate listing of things, specifically familiar to Juliette Drouet and to Hugo, is prompted by the desire to conjure up the past that is no more. But the poet's present frame of reference as he views the nature setting prevents him from resurrecting the past successfully. This idea is brought forth in the sixth strophe; only his thoughts attempt to fly on wounded wings—they, like the dead leaves on the ground which the poet moves with his feet will never become green or alive again.

> Les feuilles qui gisaient dans le bois solitaire,
> S'efforçant sous ses pas de s'élever de terre,
> Couraient dans le jardin;
> Ainsi, parfois, quand l'âme est triste, nos pensées
> S'envolent un moment sur leurs ailes blessées,
> Puis retombent soudain.

["The leaves which were strewn on the ground of the solitary woods, trying under his feet to rise from the ground, flurried about in the garden; thus, sometimes, when the heart is sad, our thoughts take flight for a moment on their wounded wings, then fall down again, suddenly."]

Part Three (strophes eight and nine) utters the poet's plea: is he a pariah, an outcast? The answer is provided him in strophes ten through fifteen which constitute the fourth part of the poem. Nature has changed; the poet recalls the past situation and attempts to relate it to the present; the idea of change is reiterated and effectively conveyed by the repetition and the variations on the single word, change. Part Five, beginning with strophe fifteen introduces the theme of death within the natural setting which undergoes continual change. The reminder "For no one here on earth ever ends or achieves the changes" imparts the final message of "Tristesse d'Olympio:" death ends everything; we all awaken at the same place in the dream. What nature has given to the two lovers, nature has taken from them.

"Tristesse d'Olympio" achieves through the clever counterpointing of negations and affirmations a novel interpretation of the passing of time. Nature is but an externalization of the human psychological process. In his aging maturity, man recalls in sadness the extinguishing dream of the romantic love he experienced when he contemplates the scene of his experiences. But he realizes that nature, however sympathetic it may have appeared to him at the moment of earlier happiness, will not bear witness for him. Hugo concludes with the thought that man has no need of nature to safeguard and preserve his experience. The essence of the experience, abstracted through time, lies in the heart of man. Remembrance is sweetened and ripened by his reminiscence; in a sense, he has vanquished both time and nature since the memory of his romantic love finds its lasting crystallization within himself.

Despite its obvious length, the love poem preserves its unity of thought and theme development. The poet's predilection for antitheses to impart his thoughts is given prominent display in the poem. Technically, "Tristesse d'Olympio" reveals Hugo's special talent for varying the rhythm of his verses to correspond or harmonize with the various shadings in the theme that is expressed. Hugo breaks the traditional caesura of the alexandrine with frequent irregularity in order to vary his rhythms and fit them to the moods of the individual strophes of the poem.

"Fonction du poète" and "Sagesse" ("Wisdom"), strategically placed at the beginning and at the end of *Les Rayons et les Ombres*, underscore the social and metaphysical dimensions already perceptible in

Hugo's poetical creed by 1840. The two poems may be considered as part of the elaborate theoretical amplification that dictated the nature of Hugo's later and best-known verse. Like the "Moïse" of Vigny, "Fonction du poète" and "Sagesse" asserted the poet's superiority, but unlike Vigny, Hugo tended to view the resultant isolation experienced by the poet less dramatically and more constructively. The poet's momentary withdrawal from the tainted limitation of society afforded him the opportunity to communicate with the forces of nature in order to decipher the secret mysteries of the universe. Such a sense of isolation was permeated with the poet's burning desire to solve the enigma of human destiny and summarily dismissed the haughty and disdainful aloofness advocated by Chateaubriand's *René*. Hugo's poet has more in common with Senancour's protagonist, *Obermann*, who explained his withdrawal from society in the following terms: "I do not wish to enjoy life, I want to hope, I would like to know." [5] With Lamartine's "Réponse à Némésis" ("Answer to Nemesis") (1831), "Fonction du poète" hurled a blanket condemnation of the purely egotistical stance advocated by René who does not seek to understand men:

> Dieu le veut, dans les temps contraires,
> Chacun travaille et chacun sert,
> Malheur à qui dit à ses frères:
> Je retourne dans le désert!
> Malheur à qui prend ses sandales
> Quand les haines et les scandales
> Tourmentent le peuple agité!
> Honte au penseur qui se mutile
> Et s'en va, chanteur inutile,
> Par la porte de la cité!

["God wishes that in troubled times everyone must work, everyone must serve. Woe on him who tells his brothers: I am returning into the desert! Woe on him who takes up his sandals when hatred and scandal torture a beleaguered people! Shame on the thinker who mutilates himself by going away outside the gates of the city, a useless singer of songs!"]

Unlike Vigny, but more like Lamartine, Hugo invests a religious or metaphysical ingredient into the poet's function. Nature, as a direct manifestation of God, remains the poet's greatest source of inspiration. The poet's enthusiasm for nature enables him to read and decipher the divine answer to the mysteries of the universe; thus, he becomes the Orphic interpreter of the earth for his fellow man.[6] Hugo speaks of the poet's communion with nature in the first part of "Fonction du poète" as the divine bow of the great lyre. This relationship is, of course, intuitively felt and experienced by the poet. Of technical interest is Hugo's increasing reliance upon the technique of antitheses to delineate the theme and message of his poem. The use of such categorical language is to a large extent related to the reassurance with which his poetical creed endows him. There can be no mistaking the function of the poet: he must become the leader of the people, the prophet, and fashioner of the new society that must be created; in Hugo's own words, the poet is the man of utopias who, like the prophet, shares in the comprehensive vision that must guide humanity. Unlike his fellow man, his eyes pierce the veils of an inner, superior vision that he shares with God. The poem, "Sagesse," bearing the subtitle, "A Mademoiselle Louise B.," links the poet's function with that of the prophet:[7] the poet's destiny is to become a thinker, to be a magus and a king, to be the alchemist who from nature and the world extracts God and reveals him to the people.

Despite his increasing awareness of the social and political problems that beset France during the 1830's and 1840's, Hugo resisted committing himself in outright fashion to any specific position until August 1848 when he openly campaigned in his newspaper,

L'Evénement, in behalf of Louis Napoleon's candidacy to the presidency of the Second Republic. The failure of his play, *Les Burgraves* (March 1843) left him disgusted with the French theatre and he published little or nothing during the years immediately following. The tragic loss of his daughter, Léopoldine, who drowned as a result of a boating accident at Villequier on her honeymoon trip with her husband, Charles Vacquerie, on 4 September of the same year drained Hugo of his literary ambitions and energies for many months. Named a peer of France in 1845, he became more absorbed with the political destiny of France, assuming moderately liberal views. Elected mayor of the Eighth *Arondissement* in Paris during 1848, Hugo became the champion of the poor and the oppressed, pronounced himself against capital punishment, and advocated freedom in education. At work on his monumental social novel, *Les Misérables,* Hugo soon detected in the president of the Republic for whom he had campaigned a dangerous usurper of power. Seven months prior to the *coup d'état* of December 1851, Hugo's newspaper, *L'Evénement,* was ordered confiscated by the reigning prince, Louis Napoleon. Such an unexpected reprisal confirmed Hugo as a staunch apostle of liberal republicanism and inspired his vituperative attack upon the emperor, *Après Auguste, Augustule* (*After Caesar Augustus, little Augustus*) later in that year. His declared opposition to the emperor, crystallized in his membership on the *Comité d'insurrection,* ended in his official expulsion from France in January of 1852. Fleeing at first to Brussels, Hugo finally found refuge on the island of Jersey (1852–55), then on the nearby Channel island of Guernsey (1855–70), where he, his family, and Juliette Drouet lived separated from their native France. Far from distracting him to the point of inactivity, the eighteen years of exile endured by Hugo confirmed and reinforced his sense of purpose and mission as a writer. At the urging of his friend, Pierre

Leroux, he solemnly and formally resolved to dedicate all of his literary efforts to the service of humanity. The exile years inspired Hugo with the kind of fervor and intensity, heretofore absent in his earlier poetical collections, that won for such volumes as *Châtiments, Les Contemplations* and *La Légende des siècles* a place of true distinction in French and western European lyricism during the nineteenth century.

The reign of Louis Napoleon III as second Emperor of France during the years 1851–70 struck a death blow to the French social Romanticists whose works advocated progress and humanitarianism. The strictly imposed censorship during the 1850's left such writers little choice: they could either accept exile and continue their moral and social preachments on foreign territory, or they could withdraw into relative quiet and isolation and practice the kind of literature that posed no threat to the newly-established status quo of the Second Empire. With the exception of such writers as Hugo, Pierre Leroux, and Emile de Girardin, the greatest majority of Romanticists elected to remain in France, diverting their literary talents in the Parnassianism developed by Théophile Gautier and the staunchest advocates of art for art's sake. From his house overlooking the sea in Guernsey, Hugo held to the Saint-Simonian conception of the social function of poetry, complicating his aesthetic creed with his personal notion of the prophetic power of the poet who was both the new priest and magus. His attraction to the magetism, illuminism, and spiritualism, rampant in certain literary circles in the 1840's and 1850's,[8] was destined to endow his lyricism with greater urgency and intensity than had been manifested before his exile in 1851.

Composed at Jersey during 1852 and 1853,[9] *Les Châtiments*, Hugo's collection of violently effective attacks upon Louis Napoleon and the Second Empire, must be regarded as an impressive masterpiece of satirical lyricism. *Les Châtiments* translate the poet's

howling scorn for the Emperor whose blatant usurpation of power in 1851 divested France of her freedom
and condemned Hugo to the excruciating pain of exile
from his native land. Hugo's anger, as it finds expression in the various pieces that constitute *Les Châtiments*, betrays his personal revulsion against the
nephew of Napoleon I as well as the anguish and
frustration that he experiences over the scandalous
curtailment or deprivation of civil liberty in the
France of the Second Empire. The epic and lyrical
elements so prominently evident in *Les Châtiments*
combine with the obvious political satire to make of
the work the greatest and fullest expression of Hugo's
talent as a poet up to this point. There can be no
serious questioning of the author's sincerity of intention and the truthfulness of his expression in the many
violent and often vituperative satirical poems in the
collection. Even a cursory reading of the satires conveys the impression of intensity of feeling and emotion that doubtlessly dictated most of the poems. We
are far from the amusing mockery of Voltaire in this
collection; there can be no mistaking the fury that
inspires the poet's attacks against everyone and everything that is symbolically associated with the regime
of Napoleon III. The object of Hugo's derision is far
from limited to the person of the Emperor; generals,
clergymen, politicians, and writers who by their ac-
tions or silence acquiesced in the dictatorship bear the
brunt of Hugo's often brutal attacks.

Part Four of the section entitled, "Ainsi les plus
abjects" ("Thus, the Most Contemptible Ones"),
characterizes the kind of lyricism underlying the often
very angry and vituperative satire of *Les Châtiments*.
Hugo's conviction that France's progress has been
cruelly and arbitrarily thwarted by the usurpation of
Louis Napoleon's power with the proclamation of the
Second Empire in 1852 is conveyed with sustained
explicitness throughout the section, so much so, in
fact, that the poet's anger appears situated or influenced by an almost hallucinatory setting of hysteria

and disorder. Hugo refers to a situation that has today
fallen into the realm of history; his poem recalls events
that appear more colored by the power of his imagination than by the facts revealed in existing records.
There can be no denying the effectiveness of his satirical comments since they are so inextricably intertwined with his own strong emotions and reactions.
The author's invective embraces in somewhat devas-
tating language all those who by omission or commis-
sion allowed the Second Empire to be proclaimed.
Hugo refers to the plebiscite of 2 December 1852 and
decries the fear, greed, and stupidity that motivated or
intimidated the will of the people to approve and
proclaim the Empire of Napoleon III. "Ainsi les plus
abjects" rails at the perpetrators of the downfall of
France without the slightest restraint or exception.
The section may be considered as a huge antithesis
between the forces of evil, delineated with such categorical denunciations, and the forces of good, conspicuously absent but implied in the tremulous words
of the satirist himself:

> *Ils ont voté!*
> *Troupeau que la peur mène paître*
> *Entre le sacristain et le garde champêtre,*
> *Vous qui, pleins de terreur, voyez, pour vous manger,*
> *Pour manger vos maisons, vos bois, votre verger,*
> *Vos meules de luzerne et vos pommes à cidre,*
> *S'ouvrir tous les matins les machoires d'une hydre;*
> *Braves gens, qui croyez en vos foins et mettez*
> *De la religion dans vos propriétés;*
> *Ames que l'argent touche et que l'or fait dévotes;*
> *Maires narquois, traînant vos paysans aux votes;*
> *Marguilliers aux regards vitreux; curés camus*
> *Hurlant à vos lutrins: Daemonem laudamus;*
> *Sots, [. . .]*
> *Invalides, lions transformés en toutous;*
> *Niais, pour qui cet homme est sauveur; vous tous*
> *Est-ce que vous croyez que la France, c'est vous,*
> *Que vous êtes le peuple, et que jamais vous eûtes*
> *Le droit de nous donner un maître, ô tas de brutes?*

["They have voted! Oh! Flock which is brought to pasture in fear under the direction of the church sexton and the village policeman, you, who are filled with terror, just look at the great jaws of the hydra open wide every morning to devour you, your homes, your woods, your orchards, your lucerne millstones, and your cider apples; good people, who believe in your farmlands and who so conveniently append religion to your sense of property; souls that are affected by the sight of money and whose devotion is increased by gold; bantering mayors, dragging your peasants to the voting place; Councilmen with glassy stares; snub-nosed priests howling in your pulpits: *We praise the Devil*; fools, [. . .] invalids, lions transformed into bowwows; simpletons, for whom this man is a redeemer, all of you, do you think, really, that you represent France, that you are the people, and that you ever possessed the right to give us a master, you bunch of animals?"]

The three hundred and eighty six lines that constitute "L'Expiation" ("The Atonement") illustrate Hugo's remarkable talent for blending satire with epic elements. Although completed in 1852, "L'Expiation" is to a large extent a reworking of Hugo's earlier speech denouncing Louis Napoleon in July of the preceding year, "What! After Caesar Augustus, little Augustus! / What! Just because / We Have Had the Great Napoleon, / Must We Now Have Napoleon the Little One!" On the surface, the poem, in true epic fashion, recalls the exploits and the destiny of Napoleon. Although Hugo speaks in admiring terms about the first Napoleon, he ascribes his need for atonement to the fact that his coup d'état during the Revolution deprived France of its civil and political liberty. The contrasts with Napoleon III are in ample evidence; compared to the magnitude of his uncle's accomplishments, Louis Napoleon and his empire of 1852–70 appear as a lamentably ironic parody of the great Napoleonic era that opened the nineteenth century. Hugo deftly evokes the great army in the cruel snows of Russia, and the defeat suffered at Waterloo as well as Napoleon's death at Saint-Helena. In Hugo's poem, the great Emperor is made to question God if the various defeats he has experienced are a form of chastisement for whatever sins he may have committed against mankind. A voice from the shadows assures him that his downfall does not constitute the atonement that he must endure to repair the evil that he may have committed. Napoleon awakens from the dead, finally, to receive the chastisement reserved for him: the realization that his name and his fame is ignominiously exploited by his nephew. The last section of "L'Expiation" affords Hugo the opportunity to catalogue his scorn and contempt for the Second Empire. The juxtaposition of the two Napoleons is both clever and effective, since the life and the deeds of each serves as an antithesis to the other. Too, the poet of "L'Expiation" is enabled to voice his condemnation of authoritarianism with considerable dramatic effect by describing the downfall of the former and predicting the forthcoming demise of the latter. At the same time, Hugo's venemous hatred for Louis Napoleon accounts for much of the emotional lyricism. Again, the poet's personal reaction leads him to construct his epic-satire with striking metaphors and antitheses, as in the following lines:

> *Ton nom leur sert de lit, Napoléon premier.*
> *On voit sur Austerlitz un peu de leur fumier.*
> *Ta gloire est un gros vin dont leur honte se grise.*

["Napoleon I, they use your name for a bed. We can see in Austerlitz a bit of their manure. Your glory is a great wine by which their shame becomes fuddled."]

Hugo is at his best in *Les Châtiments* when he depicts the present by evoking events of history with epic touches. His talent, made obvious in such successful pieces as "L'Expiation," predicts the effectiveness of his unfinished epic, *La Légende des siècles*. His propensity for amplification and exaggeration enables him to conceive of his heroes in nearly superhuman terms physically as well as morally; his Napoleon in "L'Expiation," for example, is a highly idealized conception of the historical figure, much more in tune with the poet's vivid imagination than rooted in fact or acceptable documentation. Conversely, his enemies, such as they are evoked in *Les Châtiments*, are portrayed as cruel monsters and emerge more as hallucinatory figures than as credible persons. The presentation that results is a strangely impressive blend of lyrical and epic satire that helps us to understand the nature of Hugo's conception of Romanticism. The fury and rage expressed against Louis Napoleon and his regime is sporadically relieved by confessional poems of considerably less violence which underscore more directly Hugo's sense of loss and suffering in his long exile from his native France. "Chanson," composed in Jersey in 1853, is the poet's mournful reverie of a France that he knew in earlier days. Such lyrical expression of his nostalgia for his country fits neatly in the overall pattern of *Les Châtiments*: it recalls the ills of the Second Empire with more subtlety and indirection and lends variety to the collection of poems decrying the reign of Louis Napoleon:

> . . . *Je meurs de ne plus voir les champs*
> *Où je regardais l'aube naître,*
> *De ne plus entendre les chants*
> *Que j'entendais de ma fenêtre*
> *Mon âme est où je ne puis être.*
> *Sous quatre planches de sapin,*
> *Enterrez-moi dans la prairie.*
> *—On ne peut pas vivre sans pain;*
> *On ne peut pas non plus vivre sans la patrie.—*

[". . . I die from not being able to see the fields where I used to watch the dawn rise, from not being able to hear the songs that I used to hear from my window.

My heart is where I cannot be. Bury me under four
planks of pine in the prairie. One cannot live without
bread; one cannot live either without his country."]

Les Châtiments illustrates Hugo's strengths and
weaknesses as an artist. The great variety of expression
in the poems attests eloquently to his technical genius,
but the almost excessive venom detectable in many
instances unveils the weaknesses evident in his own
character. Although his images and his metaphors
strike the reader with stunning force, they also serve as
a constant reminder that the views and arguments
presented are so exclusively and narrowly dependent
upon the poet's single-minded reactions. Were it not
for the dazzling display of poetic versatility so prominent in *Les Châtiments*, the collection, taken in its
entirety, would likely have disintegrated into a monotonous litany of complaints and accusations. The kind
of Romantic lyricism so evident in the volume stems,
in part, from Hugo's exalted sense of indignation
which, at certain intervals, suggests an effacement of
time and space. At such moments, *Les Châtiments*
translates unquestionably profoundly-felt emotions
which by stirring recollections of the past excite the
creation of intense lyricism at the moment of
composition.

When *Les Contemplations* were originally published
in two volumes in 1856, the first volume bore the title,
Autrefois (*In Times Past*), and the second, *Aujourd'hui* (*Today*). Hugo explained in his preface [10]
that the poems presented in the first volume were the
result of his poetic efforts prior to the tragic death of
his daughter, Léopoldine, in 1843, and that the poems
included in the second volume recorded directly or
indirectly his reactions to the event during the following twelve years. The poet's claim is more interesting
than it is wholly reliable; at least, it reveals the domi-
nant source of inspiration for his most universally ac-

claimed collection, *Les Contemplations*. The same preface discusses the basic thematic structure of the six books that comprise the collection: "It begins with a smile, continues with a sob, and ends with a resounding clamor of the bugle arising from the abyss." The first three books, "Aurore" ("Dawn"); "L'Ame en fleur" ("The Budding Heart") and "Les Luttes et les rêves" ("Struggles and Dreams") are often successful evocations of happy experiences and balanced meditations on human suffering; many of the poems assume the various forms of narratives, descriptive tableaux, elegies, and songs, as well as moral and didactic pieces that recall Hugo's earlier *Les Voix intérieures*. The last three books, especially "Pauca Meae" ("A Few Verses for Mine," Hugo's dead daughter, Léopoldine) and "Au Bord de l'infini" ("At the Edge of the Infinite"), Books Four and Six respectively, reveal a lyricism and a philosophical dimension unmatched in the poet's entire literary production. Hugo's expression of grief over the death of his daughter and his protest against his forced exile become welded to metaphysical considerations which make of *Les Contemplations* the most compelling collection of French Romantic poems.

In September of 1853, Madame de Girardin, the former Delphine Gay, introduced the grieving Hugo and his family to the turning tables or the ouija boards that issued messages from beyond the grave through the efforts of mediums. Prior to 1853, again through the intermediation of Madame de Girardin, Hugo had already attracted the attention of the illuminist-artist, the former priest, Alphonse-Louis Constant, better known by his pseudonym, Eliphas Lévi, who attempted to prove that cabalistic doctrine was at the root of all occult thought.[11] Gustave Simon describes the 11 September 1853 séance in the living room of Marine-Terrace when Hugo and his family believed they made contact with the deceased Léopoldine. Several other attempts at contact were made in which

Hugo transcribed the messages he thought had been communicated to him. Nor was contact established only with Hugo's daughter; the poet of *Les Contemplations* believed he communicated with the spirits of Moses, Shakespeare, and Luther as well as a variety of somewhat lesser known historical figures.[12] Gwendolyn Bays points out that the séances were not resumed after Hugo was forced to leave Jersey for Guernsey in 1855, presumably on the order of the poet's doctor who feared that his patient's mental health would become severely endangered by his persistence in such activities. Whatever else, these experiences with the voices and spirits from the great beyond provided Hugo with the assurances necessary for him to evolve the tenets of his newly-found religion in which he assumed the role of priest and magus. Declarations of his new religiosity appear in such collections as Books Four and Six of *Les Contemplations, Dieu,* and *La Fin de Satan.*

There can be little doubt that Hugo's brushes with the occult forces of spiritualism and the ouija boards are responsible for the amplification and the intensification of his conception of the poet's function after 1853. Not only is the emotional quality in the poems concerning his deceased daughter charged with greater poignancy and authenticity, but there is also ample evidence of Hugo's growing need to expand the scope of his poetic vision in the first three books of *Les Contemplations* as well.[13] His experiences with occult forces rescued Hugo from the despair and discouragement brought on by his exile, and they provided him with the sense of direction that enabled him to assert himself with sustained assurance. The knowledge that had been revealed to him during the spiritualist séances convinced him that he had found at last the key to the mystery of the universe. This secret he wished to convey to his fellow man by assuming the role of a prophet, elected specifically by God, to collaborate in the work of making known the way to man's redemption. The twenty-sixth poem, found in Book Two, entitled "Crépuscule" ("Twilight"), allegedly completed in August of 1854, is one of the more obvious attempts on the part of Hugo to reach out for the kind of supra-terrestrial knowledge provided him in such séances.

"Crépuscule" is ostensibly a meditation on the nature of human love. Hugo's contemplation of love takes place on an absolute level since he strives to balance it with the idea of death and the complete destiny of man. The first lines plunge the reader immediately into the unreal setting of the supernatural world:

> L'étang mystérieux, suaire aux blanches moires,
> Frissonne; au fond du bois la clairière apparaît;
> Les arbres sont profonds et les branches sont noires;
> Avez-vous vu Vénus à travers la forêt?

["The mysterious pond, a shroud for the watery substances, shivers; in the depths of the woods a clearing appears; the trees are thick and the branches are black; have you seen Venus anywhere in the forest?"] The title, "Twilight," announces mystery, and the alexandrine lines aptly convey the sense of gravity that permeates the poem. The setting is rather one of a séance: "shroud" carries with it a suggestion of the dead, and the luminous quality perceptible in the undulating white moires conveys the idea of life within the shadows and points to the possible presence of spirits. This strophe portrays something considerably more than the poet's melancholia; the question posed in the fourth line, "Have you seen Venus?," translates the nature of Hugo's vision: he wishes to know and so he asks the question that will penetrate the secrets of the unknown. To an extent, we may characterize "Crépuscule" as a visionary or hallucinatory poem; we may detect the fusion of material and spiritual elements as the poet's attempt to bridge the gap between the known visible world and the mysterious invisible world of the dead. Nor is matter simply relegated to the natural order in Hugo's poem: the highly imaginative use of images succeeds in suggesting such an ethereal setting that the imagery becomes a part of the vision itself—the invisible, spiritual world made visible. The thickness of the trees and the black branches, Hugo's setting for the lovers who are walking, issue a call beyond the visible reality to the unreal or supernatural world suggested by the "shroud" and the "watery white substances."

The secret of God is revealed to the two lovers by the blade of grass encountered in the third stanza. Nature as represented by the blade of grass is transformed by Hugo into a supernatural agent which becomes the main protagonist in this visionary poem. The poet, here the lovers, enters into communion with it in order to receive some kind of answer to the cosmic enigma of human life and death. The revelation contained in the first line of the fourth strophe constitutes the theme of "Crépuscule:" "God wants us to have loved." Life and death are joined only by love which provides the single, continuous line to eternity. The dead pray for the living; death transforms love into prayer. The last three strophes close the curtain to the vision: the glowworm alluded to in the fifth strophe represents the bridge between the natural and supernatural orders by evoking the countryside and by suggesting the idea of the buried ones. The torch light symbolizes love transformed into prayer after death; the grass and the tomb quiver and become silent. The revelation is completed and the hand of the supernatural draws the curtain as everything returns once again to the natural order.

> *Les mortes d'aujourd'hui furent jadis les belles.*
> *Le ver luisant dans l'ombre erre avec son flambeau.*
> *Le vent fait tressaillir, au milieu des javelles,*
> *Le brin d'herbe, et Dieu fait tressaillir le tombeau.*

["The dead women of today were the beautiful women of yesteryear. The glowworm in the shadows roams with his torch light. In the midst of the bundles of wheat, the wind causes the blade of grass to quiver and God causes the tomb to throb."]

"Crépuscule" dramatically underscores the intimately personal nature of the religiosity that resulted from Hugo's experiences with the turning tables of Jersey and the spiritualist séances of the early 1850's. Hugo's religious belief is largely dictated by his need to be consoled and reassured in his personal life. The religious beliefs that he evolved became an integral part of his poetic creed which he unhesitatingly expounded in his poems from then on. However unorthodox or extreme his views of "visions" may appear to us as they find expression in his poetic production, they are nearly always related in some fashion and to some degree to the recognizable, conventional world of reality. The fact that his religious inspiration is so directly connected with his own experience prevents Hugo from embarking with any sustained degree upon a completely hallucinated realm of the imagination. His mystical illusion always refers itself eventually, however briefly, to realistic elements which heighten the reader's fascination. There exists in such poems an immediacy or urgency of expression that makes them resemble the poetry of such modernists as Baudelaire and Rimbaud. The presence of such a visionary poem as "Crépuscule" in the second book of *Les Contemplations* points out Hugo's literary progression from the kind of carefully rearranged recollections found in his "Tristesse d'Olympio," for instance. The sense of frenzy, excitement, and immediacy which emerges from "Crépuscule" foreshadows the manner of the later French Symbolists.

It would be a gross exaggeration to assume that all of the poems in *Les Contemplations* reveal such metaphysical dimensions or display such spiritual concerns. Much of the verse signed before and after 1843 assumes the tone of simple elegy. The third poem of the section entitled, "Aurore," called simply, "Mes deux Filles" ("My Two Daughters"), is a case in point.

More than direct descriptions of his daughters, Léopoldine and Adèle, the poem is somewhat impression-
istic in that the images constitute a dreamy, moody
setting for the two girls. The familiar but clever contrast between the white carnations, the dusk, and the
butterfly suggests with effective indirectness the idea
of the charm and the delicacy possessed by the two
girls. The mood of Hugo at the writing of the poem is
injected with unobtrusiveness; as a result, the portrait
of Léopoldine and Adèle is conveyed in unusually
quiet yet eloquent terms. By contrast, such direct di-
dacticism as the lengthy "Réponse à un acte
d'accusation" [14] was meant as a reply to the charges
contained in Alexandre Duval's pamphlet that he held
a perverted influence on French letters. There can be
little mistaking the programmic tone of the piece;
Hugo defines the intention of his poetry with such
bluntness that the poem verges on the bombastic.
Ironically, the revolutionary aims of Romanticism are
defined and described in the extreme language that
characterizes his own Romantic writing.

> *Lanterne dans la rue, étoile au firmament.*
> *Elle entre aux profondeurs du langage insondable,*
> *Elle souffle dans l'art, porte-voix formidable;*
> *Et, c'est Dieu qui le veut . . .*

["A lantern in the street, a star in the firmament. She
[the literary revolution] enters into the depths of the
fathomless language, she breathes into art, the tremen-
dous megaphone, and, it is God that wishes it so
. . ."]

Book Four, entitled, "Pauca Meae," contains without a doubt the most touchingly effective lyricism in
Hugo's entire poetic output. The poems in this section
recall the memory of his daughter, Léopoldine, who
succumbed under tragic circumstances while Hugo
was on a trip in the Pyrenees in September of 1843. By
and large, the poems contain none of the despairing
and inconsolable grief which the poet is reputed to

have borne in the year immediately following the accident. The poems which constitute "Pauca Meae" are rather eloquent yet emotional meditations that evoke the memory of his daughter; they more frequently than not assume the form of simple and direct elegies. Despite the tone of relative restraint that may be discerned, the poems translate Hugo's grief in heart-rending terms whose sincerity of expression cannot be questioned. The rhythmic harmony of the majority of these verses combines with often striking imagery from which the intensity of the poet's total emotional experience may be deciphered. The father's despair over the loss of his beloved child is counterbalanced with quiet effectiveness by his heroic attempts at resignation. The sense of revolt that he experiences is ultimately assuaged by the appeasement he finally attains in such humble and quivering resignation. The poems unfold most eloquently Hugo's talent and genius as a lyricist principally because they are almost completely devoid of the pretentiousness of the verbal or pseudo-intellectual polemics that mar so much of his other verse. The poems in this section constitute one of Hugo's most distinguished poetic legacies for posterity.

Of the seventeen poems that celebrate the memory of Léopoldine, "A Villequier," composed for the first anniversary of her death, 4 September 1844, and expanded somewhat in 1846, is Hugo's most perfectly achieved expression of paternal grief. The prayerful tone of restraint and resignation invites the kind of pathos seldom elicited with such force in the poetry of Victor Hugo. The skillful alternation of the familiar stanza forms of the elegy provides the variety of rhythm necessary to sustain the emotional warmth and development of the contemplation. The juxtaposition of such different stanza forms has the effect of a counterpoint between the alternating moods of doubt, revolt, resignation, and appeasement. The poet's heavy reliance upon antitheses stems more from the nature of his inspiration and conviction than upon any willful intent to produce dazzling and startling effects. There can be no doubting Hugo's genuineness or sincerity in the poem; despite its ultimate restraint, "A Villequier" conveys the sense of catastrophic loss produced by the death of his eldest daughter. Yet the poem is not entirely freed of the poet's own idea of his importance as an educator of the masses, even though, admittedly, the apostrophe is convincingly enough joined to the main theme of the elegy to prevent it from attaining any overbearing dimension.

Je vous supplie, ô Dieu! de regarder mon âme,
     Et de considérer
Qu'humble comme un enfant et doux comme une femme,
     Je viens vous adorer!

Considérez encor que j'avais, dès l'aurore,
Travaillé, combattu, pensé, marché, lutté
Expliquant la nature à l'homme qui l'ignore,
Eclairant toute chose avec votre clarté;
Que j'avais, affrontant la haine et la colère,
     Fait ma tâche ici-bas,
Que je ne pouvais pas m'attendre à ce salaire . . .

["O God! I beg you to look into my soul, and to consider that, with the humility of a child and the gentleness of a woman, I come to worship you! Consider again that, from the dawn, I have worked, fought, thought, marched, struggled, explaining nature to man from whom it escapes, illuminating everything with your light; that, confronting hatred and anger, I had accomplished my duty here on earth, and that I could not expect this reward . . ."] Like the poems, "Trois Ans après" ("Three Years After") and "Mors" ("Death"), "A Villequier" translates what Pierre Moreau has termed the "positive force" of the human memory and imagination which has produced in "Pauca Meae" the reflection of Hugo's richly complicated soul state.

Like the majority of the Romantic poets, Hugo considered the forces of nature as the expression of the

will of God which revealed crucial secrets of the meaning of the universe to man. The poem, "Mugitusque
Boum" ("The Boom of the Oxen"), the title and
theme of which is partly inspired by Vergil's *Georgics*,
is the lyrical expression of Hugo's belief that the principle of love is contained within the bosom of the
animate and inanimate elements of nature. In "Mugitusque Boum," it is the voice of the oxen that teaches
man: "To love unceasingly, to love always, and to love
again." The inspiration of the piece may be easily
traced to Hugo rather than to Vergil who is indirectly
extolled. The statement of Hugo's personal vision of
the universe is readily discernible: man tends to be
dominated by nature into which he gradually becomes
absorbed whereby he is enabled to achieve his own
self-definition.

Hugo's experiences with the occult forces and spiritualism at Jersey during 1853 further complicated and
deepened his conception of the poet as prophet or
magus, an idea that he had suggested in *Les Voix
intérieures* of 1837 and which had been shared, in
varying degrees, with most of the French Romantic
poets. The seven hundred and ten lines that comprise
"Les Mages," completed in April of 1855, describe the
function and responsibility of the poet as interpreter
of the voices of God, Nature, and Humanity. Again,
the assurances of the superiority of the vision which
Hugo believes he possesses, thanks to his spiritualist
conversations with the great men of history, leave
their imprint upon the seventy-one strophes by conveying the immediacy of an impression or experience
rather than the balanced or ordered refashioning of a
past emotion or feeling. The theme of "Les Mages"—
that the superior man, the thinker, the scholar must
through the articulate expression of their genius guide
humanity toward its betterment and solve the most
pressing enigmas of the universe—announces the
tenor of Hugo's unfinished, yet nevertheless, monumental epic, *La Légende des siècles*. The almost inter-

minable listing of the eighty names approved by the poet as priests intermediary between God and mankind is a fairly comprehensive review of the world's greatest artists, scientists, and scholars up to the time. The thirtieth strophe speaks of the poet's inherited gift from God to decipher the mysteries of nature for his fellow man; despite its programmic appeal, Hugo's talent as a lyricist is still very much in evidence:

> *Comme ils regardent, ces messies!*
> *Oh! comme ils songent, effarés!*
> *Dans les ténèbres épaissies*
> *Quels spectateurs démesurés!*
> *Oh! que de têtes stupéfaites!*
> *Poètes, apôtres, prophètes,*
> *Méditant, parlant, écrivant,*
> *Sous des suaires, sous des voiles,*
> *Les plis des robes pleins d'étoiles,*
> *Les barbes au gouffre du vent!*

["How they gaze, these messiahs! Oh! how they think, bewildered! in the thickening darknesses, what inordinate spectators they are! Oh! what astounding heads they have! Poets, apostles, prophets, meditating, speaking, writing, under shrouds, under veils, the folds of their gowns are filled with stars, their beards are filled with the abyss of the wind!"] The collaboration between the magus-prophet and God which Hugo implies in "Les Mages" as well as elsewhere in *Les Contemplations* is momentarily challenged by the poet himself when he decreed the following formula to his fellow poets so that in times of stress they might affirm their wills to the acquisition of truth whatever the cost: "He must steal the eternal fire from the austere heavens, conquer his own mystery and steal from God." When the poem, "Ibo" ("I Shall Go"), was first published in *Les Contemplations*, the poet was decried for his haughtiness and audacity.[15] Hugo's intention was misunderstood, for "Ibo" was meant as an affirmation of the poet's resolve to persist in his lonely quest for knowledge and truth. If the poem is seen as an expression of the defiance, such as we find in the poems of Baudelaire and Rimbaud, for example, it is important to observe that Hugo chooses to emphasize in his poem the constructive aspect of the poet's willful alienation from convention and tradition. The *poètes maudits* of the Parnassian and Symbolist schools emphasized, by contrast, the sense of decadence and disintegration experienced by the poet as a result of his revolt.

"Ibo" leads logically to "Ce que dit la Bouche d'ombre" ("What the Voice from the Abyss Decrees"). The seven hundred and eighty-six lines that comprise this long poem provide us with a summation of Hugo's somewhat cosmogonic solution to the fundamental problems besetting man. Most likely completed in 1854 and presented as the poet's philosophic conclusion to the six books of *Les Contemplations*,[16] "Ce que dit la Bouche d'ombre" makes it plain that Hugo's alleged communication with the spirits of the departed at Jersey confirmed the views that he expounded in his poetry. Despite the pseudo-metaphysical intentions of "Ce que dit la Bouche d'ombre," the powerful manipulation or transposition of ideas with striking imagery rescues this impressive piece from any kind of overbearing pretentiousness and bequeaths to it a memorable lyrical quality. Hugo's cosmogonic system is an entirely personal one, dictated by his own need to assuage the grief and despair engendered by the death of his daughter, and his banishment from France by Louis Napoleon and the regime of the Second Empire. The poem is in fact a treatise on the problem of death and the destiny of man after death. Hugo evolves his own conception of eternity and links it to the origin and nature of evil in the universe. Rejecting the view that punishment, like reward, is something eternal, he explains evil as something heavily engrossed in matter that aspires through human and temporary forms of chastisement to the perfection of the spirit; he establishes the uninterrupted

chain of beings wherein the deceased evil doers may
expiate their wrongs. Hugo's conception of the trans-
migration of souls in the universe causes him to see
nature through the magnified vision of hallucination.

Oh! que la terre est froide et que les rocs sont durs!
Quelle muette horreur dans les halliers obscurs!
Les pleurs noirs de la nuit sur la colombe blanche
Tombent; le vent met nue et torture la branche;
Quel monologue affreux dans l'arbre aux rameaux verts!
Quel frisson dans l'herbe! Oh! quels yeux fixes ouverts
Dans les cailloux profonds, oubliettes des âmes!
C'est une âme que l'eau scie en ses froides lames;
C'est une âme que fait ruisseler le pressoir.
Ténèbres! l'univers est hagard.

["Oh! how cold is the earth and how hard are the
rocks! What silent horror resides in the hidden thick-
ets! The black cries of the night fall upon the white
dove; the wind strips and tortures the tree branch.
What a horrible monologue takes place in the tree
with the green branches! What a shudder runs
through the grass! Oh! what fixed open eyes are in the
underlying pebbles, dungeons of souls! The water saws
a soul in its cold lamina; it is a soul that causes the
wine press to trickle. Darknesses! the universe is hag-
gard."] The punishment of the wicked, however, is
terminal as Hugo cries out: "there is no eternal hell!"
Hell on earth is destined to be eventually transformed
into the Edens of heaven, and the work of the genius,
the prophet and the poet is to lead mankind slowly to
that evolution.

The beliefs expressed in *Les Contemplations* by and
large incited the poet to assume a role of leadership in
world affairs. As self-appointed arbiter, he intervened
with astonishing effrontery in domestic and interna-
tional issues to the point where he became eventually
known throughout the Western World. With all the
assurance of a patriarch, from his residence overlooking the ocean at Guernsey, Hugo addressed pleas to
the Swiss in behalf of the abolition of capital punish-

ment, encouraged the Mexicans to do battle against Napoleon III, and reminded England of its duty toward the Irish. Like the philosophy presented in *Les Contemplations*, Hugo's advice elicited the mixed reactions of its receivers. The reception of the poet's advice as well as of his latest collection of poems perhaps contains the most telling clue of the nature of his work. Whatever may be said of the vagueness of his metaphysical revelations or visions, *Les Contemplations* translates admirably the poet's complete lack of concern for the accepted criteria by which reality is judged or measured. In Books Four and Six especially of his collection, the rational substratum is meager to the point of being completely overcome by the poet's delirium and emotion. We are a long way from the reasonable epigrams of Voltaire and other exponents of the rationalist interpretation of the Enlightenment in Hugo's *Les Contemplations*. The visionary aspects, frequently conveyed with convincing sincerity, make it plain that the poet's sensitivity was considerably sharpened by the long exile and isolation endured in the Channel Islands. Much of the lyricism of *Les Contemplations* is endowed with a force that is as sweeping as it is suggestive. If the collection still commands our attention and elicits our interest, it is rather for the manner in which the principal poems are expressed than for any explicit theme or message which they may impart. For their undeniably personal strain and emotional scope, *Les Contemplations* serves as an excellent example of what we mean when we speak of Romantic poetry. For the sense of immediacy and urgency which so many of the poems convey, *Les Contemplations* serves as a valid illustration of the kind of verse that represents a transition from Romanticism to Modern poetry.

The poetic form perhaps best attuned to the Romantic mind or temper was the epic, and such French

Romanticists as Lamartine and Vigny experimented with it without succeeding in achieving any special distinction. For the more visionary Hugo, however, with a comprehensive view of humanity to relate to his readers, the epic form proved to be a challenge which he met with daring and achieved for himself, in so doing, a measure of greatness as an epic poet. Published in three series, 1859, 1873, and 1877, *La Légende des siècles* constitutes in actual fact a series of episodes or "lesser epics" which purport to commemorate the major events and institutions that have shaped humanity from the days of the Old Testament to the nineteenth century. Finally joined together in a collective edition in 1885, *La Légende des siècles* was originally meant to contain the crowning poems, *La Fin de Satan* and *Dieu* which remained uncompleted and whose fragments were published posthumously. Hugo's conception of the epic differs considerably from that of his predecessors in that like his counterpart, Lamartine, in the fragments of *Les Visions*, Hugo believed that the whole history of humanity could be achieved through the composition of individual poems linked together by a fundamental theme or thesis. *La Légende des siècles* traces the ascension of man from the darkness of ignorance to the light of progress and humanitarianism, and may be considered as a logical corollary to the apocalyptic poem in *Les Contemplations*, "Ce que dit la Bouche d'ombre." Hugo's comprehensive intention in the vast epic is perhaps best stated by himself in the 1859 preface to the First Series: "To express humanity in a kind of cyclic work; to portray it successively and simultaneously from all aspects, the historical, the legendary, the philosophical, the religious, and the scientific, all of which eventually fuse into a single and immense movement of ascension toward enlightenment."

H. J. Hunt points out that if "Ce que dit la Bouche d'ombre" revealed the secret of man as an individual, Hugo still sought to explain the unity of the human race as he saw it in history and created his epic to meet this end.[17] The many episodic poems that constitute *La Légende des siècles* are in fact bound together by three doctrinal sections that set forth the poet's interpretation of the progress of man in time. "La Vision d'où est sorti ce Livre" ("The Vision out of Which Was Born this Book"), "Le Satyre," and "Pleine Mer—Plein Ciel" ("Full Ocean—Full Sky") explain the core of Hugo's epic on humanity.

The vastness of such an enterprise afforded Hugo ample opportunity to inject into the series the degree of magnitude of his own vision of humanity. *La Légende des siècles* is underscored with the poet's own political and social views; numerous poems are little more than vitriolic attacks upon kings, princes, and emperors as the repressive forces that prevented mankind for so long from ascending to an enlightened state. Conversely, the almost purely lyrical treatment of the plight of the poor in such notable sections as "Les pauvres Gens" ("The Poor People") in the 1859 series, is striking by its eloquence. Metaphysical allusions to the mysterious, the infinite, and the supernatural abound; Hugo preaches a kind of deistic devotion to God. *La Légende des siècles* may be likened to a group of uneven tableaux or frescos, some impressive and others merely banal or childish, that often capture the sense of the picturesque. The poet's temperament is easily visible in the great canvases which he paints; his predilection for conceiving reality and super-reality in antithetical strokes is readily discernible throughout the three series of poems. Nearly everything is contrasted in terms of good and evil, darkness and light, ignorance and truth. Yet such simplicity of conception is more frequently than not overridden by his outstanding genius to invent metaphors and analogies that lend to the epic tales a sense of virtually overwhelming lyricism. Hugo's imaginative powers were well adapted to the epic genre; his tendency to magnify and amplify endows such biblical and legendary figures as Boaz and Roland, with a sense of grandiose majesty. Yet he manages to transform those elements of magic and the miraculous usually associated with the epic into highly suggestive symbols that represent the various stages in man's attempt to understand the mysteries of the universe that will enable him to ascend to light and perfection.

Among the most celebrated poems in *La Légende des siècles* that best demonstrate Hugo's talent for evoking biblical events with great vividness yet with considerable directness of expression are "Booz endormi" ("Boaz Asleep") and "La Conscience," both of them from the first series of poems published in 1859. "Booz endormi" is a beautifully achieved evocation from the *Book of Ruth* of the union of Boaz and Ruth from which was destined to emerge the lineage of David and Christ. Hugo's treatment of the biblical passage is a christianization of the Old Testament. The elliptic nature of "Booz endormi" announces rather the message of the Incarnation of the God-Man through the intercession of the race founded by Boaz and Ruth. "La Conscience" is a much more orthodox portrayal of the guilt suffered by Cain: Hugo stresses, rather, the vigilant eye of God pursuing Cain as the awakening of conscience in man.

Central to an adequate understanding of the scope and purpose of *La Légende des siècles* is the long poem, "Le Satyre" which Hugo placed alone under the multiple subheading, *Sixteenth Century: Renaissance and Paganism.* So strategically placed at the center of the three series, "Le Satyre" may be said to be the synthesis of the poet's philosophical and metaphysical doctrine. The satyr in Hugo's epic is presented as a mythological character—half-animal, half-man; he symbolizes the metamorphosis of man's ascension from matter to spirit. The Satyr, in the end, is changed into a giant, whose immense proportions are meant to suggest those of the universe itself. The Satyr's song before the gods on Mount Olympus relates the struggle of man against their tyranny for freedom and enlightenment. The spirit of man finally comes to dominate the repressive and dogmatic spirit of a useless deity. "Le Satyre" is divided into four sections, the first of which is appropriately entitled, "Le Bleu" ("The Blue") since it amusingly evokes the gods gathered on Mount Olympus before whom is brought the Satyr who had been caught observing Psyche bathing. The haughty gods condescend to forgive him for his boldness if he will sing for them. The Satyr's song constitutes the three remaining parts of the poem. Accompanying himself on the flute which he has borrowed from Mercury, the Satyr begins his song with "Le Noir" ("The Black") which narrates the creation of earth, and reiterates Hugo's favorite thesis: that from the inert and unconscious matter emerges life and the consciousness of man.[18] The second song of the Satyr, "Le Sombre," celebrates the effort of man struggling to overcome the heaviness of matter to attain enlightenment, while the third song, constituting the last part of the poem, entitled, "L'Etoilé" ("The Starred") predicts or prophesizes the ultimate success of man in his struggle to rid himself of the shackles of ignorance from the meaningless deity by the achievement of liberty. "Le Satyre" represents man's deliverance from the superstitions and the fears that have repressed his expression of freedom and have limited his quest for true enlightenment. Hugo has cleverly made his faun represent the spirit of the Renaissance with its insatiable curiosity for knowledge. In the end, the Satyr assumes the proportion of a Gargantuan giant, towering the silly gods, representing dogmatic religion, who are gathered on Mount Olympus. "Le Satyre" expresses the triumph of the spirit of enlightened man over the despotism of the narrow, binding dogmatism that stunted the growth of humanity until the Renaissance. It reveals Hugo's curious blend of the non-transformist interpretation of evolution with his personal metaphysics, partly inspired in turn by Saint-Simonian idealism; the faun sings of the genesis of man in "Le Sombre" in the following terms:

> *Oui, peut-être on verra l'homme devenir loi,*
> *Terrasser l'élément sous lui, saisir et tordre*
> *Cette anarchie au point d'en faire jaillir l'ordre,*
> *Le saint ordre de paix, d'amour et d'unité,*
> *Dompter tout ce qui l'a jadis persécuté,*
> *Se construire à lui-même une étrange monture*
> *Avec toute la vie et toute la nature . . .*

["Yes, perhaps we will see man become the law, overwhelm the elements under him, seize and twist his anarchy to the point of springing order from it, the holy order of peace, love and unity, subdue everything which formerly persecuted him, and build by himself a strange stock with all of life and all of nature . . ."]

In Hugo's estimation, the evil that is present in creation stems from its material texture; "Le Satyre" makes evil synonymous with matter, and the problem remains for man to rid himself of this imperfection before he may truly ascend to an enlightened state. As Hunt maintains,[19] the enfranchisement of man is achieved through the discovery of the laws which govern matter which enable him to harness it for his own purposes and thus allows him to follow his own destiny. The gods assembled on Mount Olympus symbolize the principle of limitation, fear, and ignorance from which the half-animal, half-man, the satyr, must free himself and mankind to permit the new reign of enlightenment. The final words of the satyr's song translate the exultation of mankind in its deliverance from the peril and darkness of ignorance.

> *Place au fourmillement éternel des cieux noirs,*
> *Des cieux bleus, des midis, des aurores, des soirs!*
> *Place à l'atome saint qui brûle ou qui ruisselle!*
> *Place au rayonnement de l'âme universelle!*
> *Un roi c'est de la guerre, un dieu c'est de la nuit.*
> *Liberté, vie et foi sur le dogme détruit!*

Partout une lumière et partout un génie!
Amour! tout s'entendra, tout étant harmonie!
L'azur du ciel sera l'apaisement des loups.
Place à Tout! Je suis Pan; Jupiter! à genoux.

["Make way for the eternal coming and going of the black heavens, of the blue skies, the noonday suns, the dawns and the evenings! Make way for the holy atom that burns or trickles! Make way for the radiation of the universal soul! A king means war, a god means the darkness of the night. Freedom, life and faith become superimposed on the destroyed dogma! Everywhere glows a light and everywhere glows a genius! Love. There will be understanding everywhere, since all is harmony! The azure-blue sky will be the appeasement of the wolves. Make way for Everything! I am Pan; Jupiter! get down on your knees."]

Except for the poems, *La Fin de Satan* and *Dieu*, published in their incomplete format after Hugo's death in 1885, Hugo's verse as typified in such collections as *L'Art d'être grand-père* (*The Art of Being a Grandfather*), published in 1877, and *Toute la Lyre* (*The Whole Song*), published posthumously in 1888, became considerably tempered and overshadowed by the earlier appearances of *Les Châtiments*, *Les Contemplations* and *La Légende des siècles*. Both *La Fin de Satan* and *Dieu* take up the message of the unfinished epic, and had they been completed by Hugo, they would likely have been inserted into the three series of poems to round out the epic cycle. *La Fin de Satan*, in a manner somewhat reminiscent of Milton and Blake, transforms Lucifer into an angel of deliverance and liberty. *Dieu* is the attainment of man's enlightenment through his containment of matter which causes the imperfection and evil of the world.

Despite his repeated claims of total and comprehensive vision of the universe, Hugo as a poet stirs the interest and enthusiasm of his readers more for the forceful and vivid manner of his expression than for the doctrines which may emanate from his poems. For the most part, his poetry represents the essence of French Romanticism. His conception or perception of knowledge transcends the rationalistic realm without however totally disregarding it in order to reach out into the intuitive and instinctive world of the subconscious as well as the conscious. Hugo's poetry invites us to strip away the restrictions dictated to us by practical reason and experience in order to view the world more directly with our emotions and our subconscious aspiration toward perfect knowledge and happiness. As such, his poetry moves in the direction of the modernism unleashed by the "acceleration of history" beginning with the French Revolution. The poetry of Victor Hugo may be viewed as a rejection of the rationalistic principle as too narrowly exclusive as an adequate guide for the acquisition of the depths of truth and wisdom. Whatever may be said of the nature of the "truths" or "visions" unveiled in Hugo's poetry, it must be admitted that his poetry does satisfy a partial need to visualize the world with more unity and homogeneity. A reading of Hugo's better verse affords us the opportunity to enrich, from time to time, with our imagination an otherwise bland and exasperating perception of the world by reason and practical experience alone.

5

Alfred de Musset
and the Poetry of Experience

In appraising the poetry of Alfred de Musset
(1810–57) as the exalted expression of romantic love
and sentiment, the unfortunate tendency has been to
interpret it almost exclusively in the light of the poet's
torrid love affair with the celebrated feminist novelist,
George Sand. Critic Emile Faguet, for example, states
the effect of the Venetian experience of 1833–34 with
Sand upon the development of Musset's poetry in
grossly simplified terms when he declares so categorically: "Before Venice, talent; after Venice, genius." [1]
Such an assertion only encourages the readers of Musset's verse to magnify the proportion of the emotional
crisis and tends to misconstrue his entire poetic production as an unabashed exposure of the intimacies of
his disastrous love experience. There can, of course, be
no denying the fact that Musset's major love poems
do allude, at certain intervals, to his love affair with
George Sand, and that such poems are indeed endowed with a far greater emotional range and depth
than those which were published prior to 1833. Yet it
would be closer to the truth to see in the best-known
love poems an expression of the torment and anguish
which all of his love experiences instill in him. The
psychology of love, such as it is revealed to us in the
so-called "Nuits" ("Nights") cycle, is so intimately
associated with Musset's aesthetic philosophy that it
cannot be successfully divorced from it. Despite occa-
sional allusions to George Sand, the poems also recall

the poet's adolescent disappointments in love and refer, at least indirectly, to his more tender and mature relationship with Caroline Jaubert after 1835. Thus, the "Nights" are much less the recollection of Musset's unfortunate affair with George Sand than they are the expression of the poet's painful conclusions on the nature of the experience of love and its remembrance.

Musset's Romanticism is rooted in the belief that love, with its attendant joys and sufferings, constitutes the greatest single source of man's inspiration since it reveals to him the significance of human existence. Musset isolates the passion of love from all other personal and social activity in order to make of it the unifying principle of life. Such a conclusion is dictated to him by his own emotional and intuitional experience. As a man, he sought out the emotional and sensual effects of the love experience because they alone were capable of providing him with an intense awareness of himself as a living being. As a poet, he sought to capture as directly and as completely as possible the expression of the intensity of his resulting passions and emotions. The poet's inspiration was something that stemmed immediately from the emotions contained within his own heart. However joyous or painful, the experience of love and its remembrance received its most lasting crystallization in the poem which survived the actual experience itself. Without the intense awareness of himself as an individual, he was incapable of composing poetry; thus any experience that induced such intensity within him was justifiable. Intensity of experience produced an intense and almost ecstatic kind of lyricism. Musset's great anguish and frustration lay in the realization that such intensity of emotion and passion could not be sustained or endured for any great length of time. As Geoffrey Brereton has so aptly put it: "He knew that his energy and his interest in life must dwindle year by year like a *peau de chagrin*." [2] The crux of Musset's aesthetic

principle is contained within the dilemma that his
energy and his time were limited and that he wished
to convey the intensity of his love experience in poetry
before his time ran out. The frequently feverish pace
of certain sections of the "Nights" may be explained
by this desire.

The independence of spirit that characterized Alfred
de Musset as a French Romantic poet could be discerned as early as 1828 when his friend, Paul Foucher,
introduced him to the *cénacle* of Charles Nodier. His
manner and his manifest indifference to the cause of
Romanticism became a source of dismay for the
staunchest advocates of the group. His notorious "Bal-
lade à la lune" ("Ballad to the Moon") was seen as an
equally clever parody on Romanticism as well as on
Classicism. His first collection of poems, *Contes
d'Espagne et d'Italie* (*Tales of Spain and Italy*), published when he was only twenty years old, reaffirmed
the poet's independent nature. Notable especially for
their technical dexterity, the poems betrayed a certain
influence of Romanticism by their intimately personal
tone and their generous sprinkling of local color. Yet
the collection was not viewed with complete satisfac-
tion by the Romanticists who distrusted Musset's
mirthful impertinence in such poems as "Mardoche,"
for example. Their suspicions were well corroborated
some six months later when Musset asserted his views
on literary schools in *Les Secrètes Pensées de Ra-
phaël* which appeared in July of 1830. Musset assumes
the impertinent tone of a young French gentleman
who mockingly brands all literary affiliations as non-
sense and establishes himself as an apostle of common
sense in literary matters.

> *Salut, jeunes champions d'une cause un peu vieille,*
> *Classiques bien rasés, à la face vermeille,*
> *Romantiques barbus, aux visages blêmis!..*

Vous qui des Grecs défunts balayez le rivage,
Ou d'un poignard sanglant fouillez le moyen age,
Salut!—

["Hail to you, young champions of a slightly old cause, well-shaven classicists, with shiny red faces, bearded romanticists, with ghastly pale faces! You who sweep the shores of the deceased Greeks, or with a bloodied dagger excavate the Middle Ages, Hail to you!"]

The truth of the matter was that Musset's conception of Romanticism ruled out any outright allegiance to literary theory as a basis for the practice of literature in general and poetry in particular. In a letter to his brother, Paul, dated 4 August 1831, Alfred de Musset defined his aesthetic creed as: "What the artist or the poet really needs is emotion. When I experience a certain fluttering of the heart when I write my verses, I feel certain that my poem is of the best quality that I can hatch." The poem, "A mon Ami Edouard B.," dated 1832, reiterated the claim of inspiration as the only principle of literary creation: "Oh! beat your breast, for therein lies the genius of inspiration!" After 1830, when his counterparts, Lamartine, Hugo, and Vigny began to redefine their positions as poets within specific political and social contexts, Musset maintained his attitude of indifference, withdrawing into a position of relative isolation from the literary mainstream of the 1830's and 1840's. Whereas such Romantic poets as Hugo and Vigny had rallied to the cause of social reform and humanitarianism, Musset was content to reaffirm his belief in the autonomy of art in the "Dédicace" to his poetic drama, *La Coupe et les lèvres* (*The Cup and the Lips that Drink from It*) in 1832.

L'amour est tout, —l'amour, et la vie au soleil.
Aimer est le grand point, qu'importe la maîtresse?
Qu'importe le flacon, pourvu qu'on ait l'ivresse?
Faites-vous de ce monde un songe sans réveil . . .

["Love is everything, love, and life in the sun. The main thing is to love, the mistress does not matter much. Of what importance is the bottle, as long as one is enraptured? Out of this world, create for yourself a dream without awakening . . ."]

Musset's interpretation of the poet's isolation has much less in common with the views of Vigny and Hugo on the matter than with the idea expounded by Chateaubriand in his narrative, René. Musset's poet is more closely related to the egotistical protagonist in Chateaubriand's short novel; like René, he is bent on the creation of dreams through the stimulation of his imagination. The passion kindled in his heart serves as a means of escape from the cares and responsibilities of the admittedly limited and tawdry world for whose reform he refuses to struggle. The sense of isolation experienced in Vigny and Hugo, it will be remembered, was that caused by their momentary withdrawal from the social and political scene in order to consult with more directness the source of their respective inspirations. Their resulting feelings of superiority and isolation paradoxically underscored the fact that all of their strength and energy were placed at the service of mankind. Musset steadfastly maintained his refusal to bring poetry to meet such aims. His attempt to transform love experiences into crystallized recollections emphasizes his fear and distrust of reality, and the conversion of experience into souvenir and remembrance must be taken as a form of selfish escapism.[3] This position of the poet's egotistical isolation from his fellow man is voiced again in Musset's prose play, Fantasio, published in 1834, when the poet-protagonist exclaims to Spark in Act I, scene 2: "It is a whole private world that each individual carries within himself." Fantasio bemoans the fact that he has almost worn out all of the sentiments and emotions, and he admits to the impossibility of renovating himself through the continuous experience of intensely-felt passion. As René Canat explains, Fantasio con-

sumes himself in self-pity and boredom.[4] His solitude
is spurred by the realization that he aspires to possess
limitless sensibilities and that he in fact is condemned
to its narrowest possession. Musset's protagonist ac-
knowledges the inability of the human imagination to
excite and provoke limitless dreams in man. Because
the externally organized world about him is a reminder of such limitations, he isolates himself in a
succession of dreams of his own making for the time
being. Such an idea of isolation is more directly related to Chateaubriand's *René*; like him, Fantasio pro-
fesses no real concern for the welfare of his fellow
man. If Musset's Fantasio seeks to escape from his
own personality, it is because of his painful awareness
that it is too limited and restricted. Musset's sense of
moral isolation, then, is nurtured only by the poet's
selfish considerations; its expression of anguish and
frustration is not tinged with the social consciousness
that endows Vigny's feeling of isolation with greater
dimension.

The poet's stated indifference to the social and political issues that besieged the 1830's and 1840's is
repeated with almost systematic consistency in the
various poems that he published during this time. The
dedication to his friend, A. Tattet, at the head of his
publication, *Un Spectacle dans un fauteuil* (*Plays to
be Read in an Armchair*), 1832, leaves little doubt on
his views concerning social Romanticism.

> *Je ne me suis pas fait écrivain politique,*
> *N'étant pas amoureux de la place publique.*
> *D'ailleurs, il n'entre pas dans mes prétentions*
> *D'être l'homme du siècle et de ses passions.*

["I do not consider myself a political writer, since I do
not profess any love for the public platform. Moreover, I do not in the least pretend to be the man of the
century and the translator of its [social] passions."]
Yet Musset did not remain entirely aloof from the
French political scene. In some vain attempts to in-

gratiate himself with the Orleanists after 1835, he wrote a number of poems of circumstance which, ironically enough, served to irritate Louis-Philippe rather than to reassure him of the poet's loyalty. A case in point is the political sonnet, "Au Roi, après l'attentat de Meunier" ("To the King, After the Attempted Assassination of Meunier"), written in December of 1836. The first tercet revealed Musset's ineptness or lack of tact as a potential aspirant to political favor; his clumsy use of the familiar form of expression with reference to the bourgeois king provoked the latter's displeasure at such an admonition as: "But be prudent, Philippe, and think about the country. Your thought is your wealth, and your body is your shield; it is time that you became as watchful over yourself as over your ideas." Characteristically enough, Musset's involvement with the more official nature of politics, however slight, was prompted by a concern over his own welfare as an individual rather than by any social or humanitarian intention.

The second canto of *Namouna*, an "Oriental tale in verse," inserted in *Un Spectacle dans un fauteuil* is perhaps the most telling revelation of Musset's conception of the art of poetry. Here, the poet defines poetry as a spontaneous conversation with the heart; indeed, art is nothing more than the crystallized expression of genuine sentiment. Such a view leads us to understand Musset's well-known reluctance to rework and reorder the presentation of his inspiration in his poems. It is no small irony that from the purely doctrinal point of view, he held much in common with the avowed aesthetics of the Parnassians or the exponents of art for art's sake, yet from the angle of the practice of poetry, he was as far removed from their nurtured conception of tightly constructed verse as were the other Romantic poets. Flaubert and Baudelaire, especially, expressed their unqualified contempt for the kind of poetics advocated in *Namouna* because it inevitably encouraged the practice of poetry uncontrolled in its expression of personal sentiment. For Musset, at least, the technical demands of art only served to stifle real emotion and destroyed the poet's initiative to capture the essence of his sentimental experiences in verse.

> *Sachez-le, c'est le coeur qui parle et qui soupire,*
> *Lorsque la main écrit, —c'est le coeur qui se fond;*
> *C'est le coeur qui s'étend, se découvre et respire,*
> *Comme un gai pèlerin sur le sommet d'un mont.*
> *Et puissiez-vous trouver, quand vous en voudrez rire,*
> *A dépecer nos vers le plaisir qu'ils nous font!*

["Know that it is the heart that speaks and sighs, when it is the hand that writes, it is the heart that dissolves itself; it is the heart that stretches itself, that exposes itself and breathes, like a happy pilgrim who has reached the mountain top. And may you be able to find, when you wish to mock our verses by dismembering them, the same pleasure that they have given us!"] A point well worth observing in this regard is that such a poetical code might induce great poetic expression only when the emotions and the passions of the poet have been sufficiently stirred. Such, for example, may be said to be the case for the four "Nights" and the "Lettre à Lamartine" and even possibly the much overrated "Souvenir" which Musset endows with a genuine intensity of emotional expression. The obvious failure of "Une bonne fortune" ("A Good Fortune"), written in 1836, and "Le treize Juillet" ("The Thirteenth of July"), composed in 1843, to cite but a few of Musset's less satisfying poems, underscores the inadequate fabric of the poet's creed. The tiresome strain of all forty-four strophes, of the embarrassing gushing forth of second-rate maudlin sentiment in "Une bonne fortune" is only matched by the exasperating flatness of tone produced in the equally long "Le treize Juillet" which purports to mourn the accidental death of the Duke of Orleans. Listen to the plea of strophes 16 and 17:

Qu'importe tel parti qui triomphe ou succombe?
Quel ennemi du père ose haïr le fils?
Qui pourrait insulter une pareille tombe?
On dit que, dans un bal du temps de Charles Dix,
Sur les marches du trône, il s'arrêta jadis.
Qu'il y dorme en repos du moins, puisqu'il y tombe.

Hélas! mourir ainsi, pauvre prince, à trente ans!
Sans un mot de sa femme, un regard de sa mère,
Sans avoir rien pressé dans ses bras palpitants!
Pas même une agonie, une douleur dernière!
Dieu seul lut dans son coeur l'ineffable prière
Que les anges muets apprennent aux mourants.

["What does it matter which political party triumphs
or succumbs? Which enemy of the father dares to
hate the son? Who could even insult such a tomb?
They say that, once at a ball during the reign of
Charles X, he stopped on the steps of the throne. May
he at least sleep in peace, since he has fallen. Alas! the
poor prince, to die in such a fashion at the age of
thirty! Without a word from his wife, a glance from
his mother, without embracing anyone with his palpi-
tating arms! Not a single agony, a warning pain! Only
God read the unutterable prayer in his heart which
the silent angels teach to the dying."] The distance
between the poet and his heart, in this instance, appears somewhat far removed, and the conversation
that is recorded, contrary to Musset's claim in *Namouna,* is more the prosaic result of the guiding hand
that writes the poem than the murmur of the heart
that speaks and sighs. The stuff from which the poet
will occasionally be enabled to achieve the "creation
of a pearl from a tearful sentiment" such as he declares in "Impromptu" is conspicuously lacking in
many such lesser poems as "Le treize Juillet."

All of Musset's lyric and satiric poetry was collected
and published during the poet's lifetime in two volumes called simply, *Premières poésies* (1829–1835)

and *Poésies nouvelles* (1836–52). When the poem, "Venise" appeared initially in the collection, *Contes d'Espagne et d'Italie*, it was hailed by the leading exponents of the *cénacle* of Nodier as a model of Romantic poetry and its author was considered to be a poet of great promise. Indeed, the unassuming facility discernible in "Venise" points to the virtuosity of expression which Musset will later achieve in his "Nights." The kind of fantasy conjured up in the poem was almost conventional in the sense that it reverberated the voguish imitations of Italy and Venice as Lord Byron had portrayed them in the last canto of his *Childe Harold*. Musset's poem is permeated with touches of local color that were certain to please the readers of the early 1830's in France. Yet the archaic and stilted language of "Venise" is not entirely devoid of a quaint charm; the young Romantic poet pulls out all of the stops in his fanciful evocation of the city: it is the Venice of stunning twilights and masked balls that is conveyed more through the poet's imagination than through any actual power of observation.

The long poem, "Rolla" which was composed in August of 1833, some weeks before his meeting with George Sand, is a curious diatribe against Voltaire and the rationalism of the eighteenth century. In design as well as in treatment, "Rolla" may be considered as an early projection of Paul Bourget's end-of-the-century novel, *Le Disciple*, which was meant as a scathing denunciation of the spirit of Positivism that had impregnated the minds of the younger generations. "Rolla" is a narrative poem that recounts the story of a young *roué*, who, experiencing an overwhelming feeling of disgust with life, takes his life after having briefly tasted genuine affection. Musset places the blame for the lack of meaningful idealism squarely on the spirit of the Enlightenment such as it was embodied in the works of one of its leading exponents, Voltaire. The poet accuses the *philosophes* of having ruthlessly supplanted religious belief by reason, thus creating a cataclysmic vacuum for those who founded the meaning of their existence in such belief. Not only does the poem reveal Musset's grossly simplified interpretation of the Enlightenment, it also points to the more orthodox interpretations of the Classical spirit that ultimately influenced both his life and work. Unlike Lamartine, Hugo, and even Vigny, who seek to rework the tenets and traditions of Christianity into a new framework to make it correspond to the needs of nineteenth-century society, Musset is content to invoke the spirit of Christianity in its more traditional conception. The attack upon the Enlightenment in "Rolla" is conducted in the most antithetical manner imaginable; the poem is riddled with emotional apostrophes, and the tremor of anger in the poet's words may be easily deciphered:

Voilà pourtant ton oeuvre, Arouet, voilà l'homme
Tel que tu l'as voulu. —C'est dans ce siècle-ci,
C'est d'hier seulement qu'on peut mourir ainsi. [. . .]
Vous vouliez faire un monde.—Eh bien, vous l'avez fait;
Votre monde est superbe, et votre homme est parfait!
Les monts sont nivelés, la plaine est éclaircie;
Vous avez sagement taillé l'arbre de vie;
Tout est bien balayé sur vos chemins de fer,
Tout est grand, tout est beau, mais on meurt dans votre
    air.

["However, Arouet, there is your work, there is man such as you conceived him to be. It is only in this century, it is only since yesterday that we can die that way. [. . .] You wanted to fashion a world. Well, you have done so; your world is superb, and the man you have created is perfect! The mountains have been levelled, the plain has been cleared; you have wisely pruned the tree of life; everything has been thoroughly swept on your railways, everything is grand, everything is beautiful, but we are suffocating to death in your air."]

In 1833, Musset met George Sand for the first time

at a dinner given by Buloz, director of the *Revue des Deux Mondes*. After a few minor overtures, the two declared their love for one another. Having spent the autumn of 1833 in a cottage at Fontainebleau, they agreed to travel to Venice together during December of the same year. There, the expression of their mutual passion for each other fluctuated; it is likely that they were too much alike and they began to compete for exclusive attention with the kind of relentlessness that was bound to doom their relationship. In February of 1834, Musset took violently ill. When the poet realized that his attending physician, Pietro Pagello, had managed to steal the affection of George Sand from him, he arranged to depart for Paris in late March in order to leave the two lovers to themselves. There, Musset wavered from moments of quiet resignation to fits of violent despair in which he was moved to attempt several reconciliations with his former mistress. The final break with George Sand occurred in March of 1835 when it became evident to both that it was futile to try to remedy the situation. Whatever else, the stormy love affair deepened the young poet's emotional experience to the point where he was now ready to compose love poems which were endowed with genuine sincerity. Musset was moved to write his greatest poetry during the short span of four years that followed. The love poems may be said to comprise a cycle of seven poems, notably: "La Nuit de mai" ("The Night in May"), written in 1835; "La Nuit de décembre" ("The Night in December"); followed by the "Lettre à Lamartine" written the following year; "La Nuit d'août" ("The Night in August") in 1836; "La Nuit d'octobre" in 1837; "L'Espoir en Dieu" ("Hope in God"), composed in 1838 and attached to the love sequence; and finally, "Souvenir," written in September of 1840. Taken individually and viewed compositely, the seven poems constitute Musset's greatest legacy to French Romantic poetry.

Like the other so-called "Nights," "La Nuit de mai"

is cast in the form of a dialogue; in this specific poem, the conversation that takes place is between the poet and his muse. Musset's idea of contrasting the poet with the muse is surprisingly effective in this instance: the two agents symbolize with singular appropriateness the two tendencies which oppose themselves in the poet, his inspiration which presses him to create, and his sense of discouragement which seeks the effacement of silence. Structurally, the alternation of the alexandrine line (to voice the optimism of the Muse) with the eight-foot line (to convey the lethargy of the Poet) produces a felicitous result. Musset possesses an instinct for rhyme; there emerges from his verse a pleasant harmony that is caused by a wide variety of musical rhythms that correspond to each variation in tone that is conveyed by the dialogue of the Muse and the Poet. The muse makes appeals to the poet, the first of which is milder and more consoling than is the second, which assumes a somewhat more severe pitch. When the poet fails to respond affirmatively to the muse's entreaties to perform, he is reminded of his duty: it is the responsibility of the poet to turn his otherwise egotistical meditation on suffering into a piercing song for God and man. The center of the poem is concerned with the narrative of the legend of the pelican which the muse recounts in order to encourage and poet to shake off his state of lethargy. The pathetic drama of the self-sacrificing pelican who, unable to feed its young, offers its body and blood as food is meant to symbolize the plight of the suffering poet. The image of the pelican feeding its young suggests the image of the poet who creates poetry out of the sufferings he endures.[5] Just as the pain transforms the pelican into a sublime animal in this instance, so too will the pain of the poet endow his work with the indelible stamp of genius. Lyrical expression that embodies the poet's personal pain and anguish cannot help but be endowed with an intensity of feeling and emotion that contrasts sharply with the flippancy and cleverness of more facile poetry. The poet's lethargic state in "La Nuit de mai" points to the drama of poetic apathy at crucial points of Baudelaire's *Les Fleurs du Mal* (*The Flowers of Evil*). The poet's lethargy is rooted in his despair and discouragement; the ability to use this condition as a subject of poetry cloaks such verse in meaningfulness:

> *Poète, c'est ainsi que font les grands poètes.*
> *Ils laissent s'égayer ceux qui vivent un temps;*
> *Mais les festins humains qu'ils servent à leurs fêtes*
> *Ressemblent la plupart à ceux des pélicans.*
> *Quand ils parlent ainsi d'espérances trompées,*
> *De tristesse et d'oubli, d'amour et de malheur,*
> *Ce n'est pas un concert à dilater le coeur.*
> *Leurs déclamations sont comme des épées:*
> *Elles tracent dans l'air un cercle éblouissant,*
> *Mais il y pend toujours quelque goutte de sang.*

["Poet, that is the procedure of the great poets. They leave to their merriment those who do not aspire to immortality; but the human banquets which they serve in their festivities resemble, for the most part, those of the pelicans. Thus, when they speak of broken hopes, of sadness and forgetting, of love and misfortune, it is not a concert meant to cheer the heart. Rather, their declamations are like swords: they outline in the air a dazzling circle, but there always hangs from it some drop of blood."]

The poet's response is at first a timid one: he agrees to let the partial echo of his anguish resound in his poetry, but ultimately, he refuses to portray the acuteness of his suffering since it is rather something that he feels and is unable to express in words. His brief retort to the muse underscores his basic fear and reticence:

> *Hélas! pas même la souffrance:*
> *La bouche garde le silence*
> *Pour écouter parler le coeur.*

["Alas! not even for suffering: the mouth keeps itself silent in order to listen to the words of the heart."]

"La Nuit de mai" ends on a note of optimism, however, with the implication that the poet has been
awakened from the passive state that prevents him
from recording his sentiments and emotions. Technically, the poem is one of Musset's greatest achieve-
ments in lyricism; the breathless pace of the dialogue
translates the poet's sweeping involvement in the topi-
cal issue at hand.

If "La Nuit de mai" unfolded the plight of the
saddened poet, unable to respond with resoluteness to
the entreaties of the muse because of the overwhelming anguish he suffered as a result of a disastrous love
experience, "La Nuit de décembre" underscores the
necessity for the poet to isolate himself so that he may
be enabled to activate his creative powers. Unlike the
other "Nights," "La Nuit de décembre" does not uti-
lize the device of the dialogue between muse and poet;
instead, the haunting presence of a strangely silent
"double" or *alter ego* [6] at the conclusion of the poem
identifies itself in a manner that is meant to reassure
the poet in his undertaking. The underlying theme of
"La Nuit de décembre" is announced in unassumingly
simple language in the first strophe:

> *Du temps que j'étais écolier,*
> *Je restais un soir à veiller*
> *Dans notre salle solitaire.*
> *Devant ma table vint s'asseoir*
> *Un pauvre enfant vêtu de noir,*
> *Qui me ressemblait comme un frère.*

["When I was a schoolboy, once I stayed awake all
night in our solitary room. There came to sit in front
of my working table a poor child clothed in black, who
resembled me like a brother."]

The specter of the unknown stranger appears with
increasingly haunting frequency as the poet undergoes
the personal and emotional experiences that constitute the milestones of his life. With each appearance,
the silent stranger imposes himself upon the mind of

the suffering poet with compelling urgency. Much of the effectiveness of "La Nuit de décembre" is derived from the slowly cadenced crescendo that builds up to the end of the poem with each appearance of the ghostly vision. In the end, its identity is revealed to the questioning poet; the silent stranger is solitude, the required condition for the poet's inspiration to materialize into poetry: "The heavens have entrusted your heart to me; I will accompany you along the road, but I am unable to touch your hand. My friend, I am Solitude."

Just as Lamartine had confessed his anguished suffering to Lord Byron, Musset now looks to Lamartine, as the poet of love and expresses the story of his thwarted hope and disillusionment in "La Lettre à M. Lamartine:"

> Qu'un instant, comme toi, devant ce ciel immense,
> J'ai serré dans mes bras la vie et l'espérance,
> Et qu'ainsi que le tien, mon rêve s'est enfui?
> Te dirai-je qu'un soir, dans la brise embaumée,
> Endormi, comme toi, dans la paix du bonheur,
> Aux célestes accents d'une voix bien-aimée,
> J'ai cru sentir le temps s'arrêter dans mon coeur?
> Te dirai-je qu'un soir, resté seul sur la terre,
> Dévoré, comme toi, d'un affreux souvenir,
> Je me suis étonné de ma propre misère,
> Et de ce qu'un enfant peut souffrir sans mourir?

["That for an instant, like you, under this immense sky, I held life and hope in my arms, and that like yours, my dream escaped from me? Shall I tell you that one evening, in the perfumed breeze, asleep, like you, in the assurance of happiness, to the heavenly strains of a cherished voice, I thought that I felt time stopping in my heart? Shall I tell you that one evening, left alone on earth, devoured, like you, by a horrible memory, I became astonished at my own wretchedness, and at what a child can suffer without dying?"] Despite its unusual length, "La Lettre à Lamartine" succeeds in sustaining the lyrical quiver that

saves it from deteriorating into a revealing exposé. The
poem may be seen as a kind of necessary therapy for
Musset; one senses the feeling of assuagement experienced by the poet as "La Lettre à Lamartine" proceeds to its exultant conclusion: "Do not complain of
yesterday, let the new dawn come; your soul is immortal, and time is running out."

"La Nuit d'août" follows "La Lettre à Lamartine"
and translates the poet's somewhat more hopeful attitude. The almost feverish pace of the poem betrays
the impossible dilemma in which the poet finds himself. He resolves to overcome his initial despair
wrought by an unhappy love affair and announces that
he will seek love elsewhere. Despite the warnings of
the muse that he may exhaust himself as well as his
experiences, the poet answers that he cannot disen-
gage himself from the passions which convey to him
the intensity of experience that he needs to write
poetry. The last poem of the "Nights" cycle, "La
Nuit d'octobre," is particularly touching for the manner in which it reviews the poet's course from despair
and disillusionment to renewed confidence and hope
in the future. In the belief that he has completely
overcome his grief, the poet begins to relate with
painstaking detail the history of his unfortunate love
affair only to find himself overwhelmed with an emotional anger that causes him to denounce the woman
he loved. The ascending pitch that the confession
takes conveys the impression of a taut, brittle drama;
the poet's reactions are so vividly recalled that they
become fused with the present. It is this ingredient
that endows the poem with its sense of immediacy
and intensity. The fitful poet is calmed finally by the
consoling words of the muse who points out the fact
that his pain has actually provided him with the
inspiration necessary to compose lasting verse:

> De quoi te plains-tu donc? L'immortelle espérance
> S'est retrempée en toi sous la main du malheur.

Pourquoi veux-tu haïr ta jeune expérience,
Et détester un mal qui t'a rendu meilleur?
O mon enfant! plains-la, cette belle infidèle
Qui fit couler jadis les larmes de tes yeux;
Plains-la! c'est une femme, et Dieu t'a fait, près d'elle,
Deviner, en souffrant, le secret des heureux.

["Of what, then, are you complaining? Immortal hope
has become steeped in you again under the hand of
misfortune. Why do you want to hate your youthful
experience, and detest an evil that has made a better
man of you? Oh! my child, pity her, this beautiful
unfaithful woman who once caused tears to gush from
your eyes; pity her! she is a woman, and God has
caused that next to her, by your suffering, you should
have guessed the secret of those who are happy."]
More than the other "Nights," "La Nuit d'octobre"
attempts to extract from the individualized experiences with women a meaningful statement on the
psychology of human love. The strange blend of joy
and agony which has overtaken the poet as a result of
his particular love affairs has afforded him a momentary glimpse of a higher and more perfect state of
happiness. The experience of love, then, is less important than the fact that one has undergone the experience which eventually becomes relegated to the realm
of memory and recollection. To have loved in the past
is more important than loving in the present. The love
experience, then, is used by Musset as a kind of tram-
poline which enabled him to soar to new heights and
catch a fleeting glimpse of the permanent kind of
happiness to which all men aspire. At the end of "La
Nuit d'octobre," the poet is ready to accept his plight
with melancholic resignation.

In an effort to escape the metaphysical anguish engendered in him by the nature of his various love
experiences, Musset composed in 1838 the long poem,
"L'Espoir en Dieu," in which he voiced his need to
reach God directly through the sentiments of his own
heart rather than through the odious and needlessly

complicated machinery of organized Christianity. As
Philippe van Tieghen asserted, "L'Espoir en Dieu" is
a logical corollary to the love poems of the "Nights"
cycle because of the fact that Musset's sentimental
crises reflected more directly a moral concern than an
emotional or sentimental one.[7] The truth of the matter was that with each love experience, Musset grew to
realize with agonizing intensity that the individual
women involved meant less to him that the experience
of love itself, which was the only thing in which he
was able to make a profession of faith. The doubts and
pains inflicted upon him by instances of unfaithful-
ness increased the anguish and degradation that he
felt because he had come to make of love his only
religion. Much less an apology for religion than the
lyrical account of his odyssey from confusion to reassurance, "L'Espoir en Dieu" is Musset's most complete expression of his romantic religiosity. Brushing
aside with sweeping generalizations the confusion be-
gotten from the various philosophical systems
throughout history, the poet counsels the philosopher
to renounce the selfish pride that incites him to seek
rational solutions to the enigmas of human destiny.
He invites his readers to kneel with him and pray for
divine reassurance. The tone of Musset's personal peti-
tion to God reveals a religiosity inspired in part by the
personal deism of Jean-Jacques Rousseau:

> Brise cette voûte profonde
> Qui couvre la création;
> Soulève les voiles du monde,
> Et montre-toi, Dieu juste et bon.
> Tu n'apercevras sur la terre
> Qu'un ardent amour de la foi,
> Et l'humanité toute entière
> Se prosternera devant toi.

["Remove this immense canopy that covers all of creation; lift the veils from the people, and show yourself
to us, good and just God! You will notice nothing but

a burning love of faith on earth, and all of humanity
will kneel before you."]

First published in the February 1841 issue of the
Revue des Deux Mondes, the poem, "Souvenir," may
be viewed in a general way as the epilogue to the
"Nights," but more specifically, it may be seen as a
kind of recollected inventory of the poet's love affair
with George Sand. The poem was inspired by Musset's passing through sections of the forest of Fontainebleau in September of 1840, scene of the more
idyllic portion of his experience with Sand, on his way
to visit a family friend, Madame Berryer, in the châ-
teau of Angerville. Some time later, the poet met his
former mistress in the lobby of the Théâtre Italien,
and was prompted to compose and finish "Souvenir."
Whatever else may be said of its genesis, the poem, by
its qualities as well as its defects, affords us the opportunity to contrast Musset's accomplishment with his
other love poems and arrive at a clearer definition of
his art as this may be seen in his major works. "Souvenir" is filled with the kind of serenity of thought and
mood that is so conspicuously lacking in the great
"Nights." As the title itself indicates, "Souvenir" is a
recollection of past events in his affair with George
Sand; the poet's souvenir, however, is dictated by a
main theme that gives the poem significantly more
order and cohesion than were achieved in the more
emotionally feverish "Nights." Yet the theme of "Souvenir" may hardly be considered as original in Musset's poetry. The idea of the superior value ascribed to
the crystallized remembrance of love over the actual
experience itself is a theme that is somehow asserted
in all major love poems as a recurrent and effective
motif. In "Souvenir," the theme is spelled out in such
clear and forthright language, nearly devoid of all
emotion, that the subtlety is lost in the forceful assertion that borders on the prosaic. The poet's consciously controlled emotion throughout the poem
strips it of the kind of sustained spontaneity so fre-

quently in evidence in such pieces as "La Nuit de mai" and "La Nuit d'octobre." The reader is constantly reminded that the events and the emotions described are relegated to the past. The final strophes of the poem are declaimed in the language that suggests the poet's triumph over incidents which he may safely place in the past:

> La foudre maintenant peut tomber sur ma tête,
> Jamais ce souvenir ne peut m'être arraché;
> Comme le matelot brisé par la tempête,
>   Je m'y tiens attaché.

> Je ne veux rien savoir, ni si les champs fleurissent,
> Ni ce qu'il adviendra du simalcre humain,
> Ni si ces vastes cieux éclaireront demain
>   Ce qu'ils ensevelissent.

> Je me dis seulement: A cette heure, en ce lieu,
> Un jour, je fus aimé, j'aimais, elle était belle.
> J'enfouis ce trésor dans mon âme immortelle,
>   Et je l'emporte à Dieu!

["Lightning can now descend upon me, never will this souvenir be taken from me; like the sailor broken by the storm, I shall hold on to it. I do not wish to know anything, whether the fields will bloom, what will happen to the human image, whether these vast skies will illuminate tomorrow what they bury today. I only tell myself: At this very time and place, one day, I was loved, I loved, she was beautiful. I shall hide this treasure in my immortal soul, and I shall take it up to God."] However excellent the therapy for Musset, "Souvenir" as a poem lacks the sense of personal involvement that characterizes his most successful verse. There lurks a strange nostalgia for the effects achieved in Lamartine's "Le Lac" and Hugo's "Tristesse d'Olympio." Musset seems to have been striving for the kind of reassurance conveyed by both Lamartine and Hugo with relationship to their respective love affairs with Madame Charles and Juliette Drouet. In theme as well as in treatment, "Souvenir" invites comparison with the abovementioned poems even though Musset's originality pushes somewhat further with the affirmation that the remembrance of the love experience is far more valuable than the experience itself. Like his two predecessors, Musset has managed, although somewhat more timidly given his background and circumstances, to isolate a meaningful experience which brought a sense of unity to his own existence. However true this may be, Musset may be reproached for removing the excitement from his poem by his recourse to such predictable language in "Souvenir." There is no imtimacy of expression or sense of anticipation that endowed some of the "Nights" with vitality and excitement. Georges Poulet has described Musset's best poetry with particular aptness when he said: "It mounts up, it bursts forth in a kind of smarting realization of not yet being what it is going to be; it is the feeling of mad impatience and of extreme thirst which one experiences at the instant when the cup has not quite yet touched the lips . . ." [8] The truth of the matter was that Musset's new-found serenity and regained confidence in 1841 played a detrimental role in the practice of the type of lyricism that had won him distinction in the cycle of the love poems. Musset's poetry after 1841 falls more readily into the category of the circumstantial and conventional than into the genuinely lyrical. His development as a poet reached its apogee in 1841; "Souvenir" reviewed the whole gamut of inspiration and the poet's reaction to it. After 1852, the poet saw fit to publish little or nothing. Like Rimbaud, we may regret also the fact that Musset appeared to suppress the real expression of his poetic genius after 1841: "Musset did not know how to do anything. There were visions behind the gauze of the curtains; he closed his eyes to them." [9]

It may be said that Musset was more of a Romanticist by temperament rather than by any strong esthetic or social conviction. For the most part, his verse preserves a respect for balance and order, qualities which had become part and parcel of the French mind since Descartes and Boileau. However sincerely and spontaneously he revealed his emotions in his best verse, he always attempted to endow his writing with the external accouterments of common sense and good measure. His personal attitude toward life, partly a result of his liberal classical upbringing, certainly contributed to making him the most uncommitted of all the French Romanticists. It was natural that his abhorrence of extremes and excesses should lead him to appreciate such qualities of restraint and balance in the works of France's greatest comedy writer, Molière. Despite Musset's tenaciously conservative views concerning the effectiveness of the rules that governed Classical tragedy,[10] he was greatly impressed by the kind of sobriety and naturalness that tempered the writings of such classicists as Molière and La Fontaine. As a poet, Musset aimed at the achievement of a similar balance in his own work, despite his frequent recourse to fantasy. His best poems, in fact, are endowed with the kind of clarity that overshadows, ultimately, whatever inconsistencies of style may be discerned. The composition in 1840 of the critical and satirical poem known as "Une Soirée perdue" ("A Wasted Evening"), made it clear that he disowned the shoddier and more dogmatic aspects of Romanticism in favor of the saner and more common-sense approach of such great writers as Molière. He is a particularly adept literary critic in "Une Soirée perdue" by managing a skillful critical appraisal of Molière's qualities with an accompanying attack upon the dramatic literature of his own time. The poem is written with almost classic understatement; "Une Soirée perdue" alludes to the boredom generated in the audience of the Comédie Française at a performance of *Le*

Misanthrope. The opening section of the poem, sar-
castically underscoring the vacuousness of the nineteenth-century Romantic mind, draws Musset logically into a discussion of the so-called "bungling" of a
comedy writer who could engender so much boredom
in such an audience. Without approaching his subject
with the tedious air of the scholar, Musset manages to
give a brilliant characterization of Molière's art as a
writer, clearly marking the seriousness of intention in
the comic form of *Le Misanthrope.* Musset champions Molière as one of France's most effective por-
trayers of human misery and deceit; Molière's propensity to speak out the bitter truth with utmost frank-
ness is described as the playwright's only passion in his
comedies. It is the seventeenth-century author's insistence on truth that alienates him from the Romantic
age, in Musset's view; in the name of such a principle,
he would avenge Molière and assume the role of Al-
ceste in the nineteenth century:

> Que c'était une triste et honteuse misère
> Que cette solitude à l'entour de Molière,
> Et qu'il est pourtant temps, comme dit la chanson,
> De sortir de ce siècle ou d'en avoir raison;
> Car à quoi comparer cette scène embourbée,
> Et l'effroyable honte où la muse est tombée?
> La lâcheté nous bride, et les sots vont disant
> Que, sous ce vieux soleil, tout est fait à présent;
> Comme si les travers de la famille humaine
> Ne rajeunissaient pas chaque an, chaque semaine.
> Notre siècle a ses moeurs, partant, sa vérité;
> Celui qui l'ose dire est toujours écouté.

["That it was a sad and pitiable shame, this solitude
around Molière, and that it is however the time, as the
song says, to get out of this century or to get the best
of it; for to what may this muddied stage be compared, and the horrible disgrace into which the muse
has fallen? Cowardice restrains us, and idiots go about
saying that everything has already been done, under
this ancient sun; as if the foibles of the human family

were not rejuvenated with each new year, each new week. Our century has its own manners, and thus, its own truth; he who dares to speak it is always listened to."]

In "Une Soirée perdue," Musset speaks in behalf of reason which he equates with the acquisition of truth. The poem is a plea to his contemporaries to return to the portrayal of the human character with the soundness of psychological penetration exhibited by Molière in *Le Misanthrope*. Musset's entreaty to the spirit of Molière to endow him with the "whip of satire" and the secret with which he can proclaim this truth in his own generation is a subtle reproach to such dramatists as Dumas père and Scribe whose fashionable well-made plays lacked lasting substance and genuine emotion.

"Une Soirée perdue" underscores Musset's predilection for classical restraint and balance. Once he had resolved his own emotional crises in the poems which constitute his most distinguished production as a poet, he reacted vigorously to the growing dogmatism of the widely accepted conception of Romanticism and reaffirmed his preference for a loosely interpreted kind of Classicism. This wavering between two diametrically opposed tendencies explains both the nature of his own Romanticism and his well-known recalcitrance in identifying himself with the movement in any active manner. His independent attitude caused him to write some of the most personal verse produced by the French Romantic poets.

Notes

1 – Toward a Definition of Romanticism

1. Voltaire, "Candide" in *Romans et contes* edited by Henri Bénac (Paris: Garnier, n.d.), p. 221.

2. "Zadig" in *Romans et contes*, p. 56.

3. See especially Book Ten of Plato's *Republic* for a discussion of the function of the poet.

4. Maurice Z. Shroder, *Icarus: The Image of the Artist in French Romanticism* (Cambridge, Mass.: Harvard, 1961), p. 21.

5. Jean Cassou, *Les Nuits de Musset* (Paris: Emile-Paul Frères, 1930), p. 7.

6. Maurice Levaillant, *Le Romantisme* in *Neuf Siècles de Littérature française* (Paris: Delagrave, 1958), p. 369.

7. *De la Littérature*, Part I, Chapter 11. Madame de Staël was not alone in making this distinction. Schlegel defended the thesis as early as 1798. The same point was also made by Benjamin Constant and Sismondi. For a fuller discussion of the issue, see Paul van Tieghem's *Le Préromantisme: études d'histoire littéraire européenne* (Paris: Alcan, 1931).

8. *De la Littérature*, Part II, Chapter 2.

9. *Ibid.*, Part I, Chapter 11.

10. *De l'Allemagne*, Book II, Chapter 11.

11. *De la Littérature*, Part II, Chapter 11.

12. *Ibid.*, Part II, Chapter 9.

13. *Ibid.*, Part II, Chapter 15.

14. In this same connection, see François René Chateaubriand's *Essai sur la littérature anglaise* (Part II), and the *Mémoires d'outre-tombe* (Part II, Book II).

15. Pierre Simon Ballanche published in 1801 his *Du Sentiment considérée dans ses rapports avec la littérature et les beaux-arts,* and Senancour's epistolary novel, *Obermann,* appeared in 1804.

16. Cf. Chateaubriand's Preface to the *Génie du Christianisme*.

17. *Le Génie du Christianisme*, Part II, Book 5, Chapter 2.

18. *René* was published as a separate narrative in 1805.

19. Charles Augustin Sainte-Beuve, *Chateaubriand et son groupe sous l'Empire* I, 344–47.

20. Chateaubriand, *René* (Paris: Garnier, 1962), p. 210.

21. *Ibid.*, p. 215.

22. Victor Hugo, *La Préface de Cromwell.*

23. *Ibid.*

24. *Ibid.*

25. *Alfred de Vigny, Stello.*

26. Alphonse de Lamartine, Preface to the *Oeuvres* published in 1834 under the title, "Les Destinées de la Poésie."

27. Preface to *Les Odes et poésies diverses*, 1822.

28. Preface to *Les Voix intérieures*, 1837.

29. Preface to *Les Rayons et les ombres*, 1840.

30. "Fonction du poète" in *Les Rayons et les ombres*, 1840.

31. Ludovic Vitet in the 2 April 1825 issue of *Le Globe*: "Such is what Romanticism is for those who understand it in its largest and most general sense, or, more precisely, from a philosophical point of view. In two words, it is a form of protestantism in art and literature."

32. "Les Mages" in Book VI of *Les Contemplations*, 1856.

33. "Ce que dit la Bouche d'ombre" in *Les Contemplations*.

34. "Bouteille à la mer" in *Les Destinées*, published posthumously.

35. Théophile Gautier, Preface to *Albertus*, 1832.

36. Hugo, *William Shakespeare*, Part II, Book VI, Chapter 1.

37. Baudelaire, *Oeuvres complètes* (Paris: Pléiade, 1954), p. 610.

2 — Lamartine and the Neo-Classical Inheritance

1. When they were first published in 1820, they were unsigned. The definitive edition of the *Méditations poé-*

tiques, edited by Gustave Lanson, was published in the series, "Les Grands Ecrivains de la France" by Hachette. For a fuller treatment of the life of Lamartine (1790–1869), consult Henri Guillemin, *Lamartine, l'homme et l'oeuvre* (Paris: Boivin, 1940).

2. See Helmut A. Hatzfeld, *L'Initiation à l'explication de textes français* (München, 1966), pp. 80–87 for an illuminating interpretation of "Le Lac."

3. The poem, "Le Vallon," for example, illustrates Lamartine's more objective observation of reality.

4. "Le Crucifix" was composed in 1823, six years after the death of Julie Charles.

5. See *Le Génie du Christianisme,* Part I, Book V for François René Chateaubriand's attempt to illustrate the existence of God through the contemplation of the marvels and beauties of nature.

6. His *Histoire des Girondins,* 1847, is a tribute to the ideal type of revolutionary. His journal, *Le Civilisateur,* and the twenty-eight volumes that comprise the *Cours familier de littérature* (1856–69), were meant to acquaint the masses with the great masterpieces of world literature.

7. D. Gallois and J.-B. Piéri, *Le Dix-Neuvième Siècle* (Paris: Eugène Belin, 1960), pp. 104–7 argue convincingly that Lamartine had first conceived of *Jocelyn* as a long pastoral poem, separate from *Les Visions.*

8. Consult the critical edition of *Jocelyn* edited by Jean des Cognets and published by Garnier (Paris) in 1960.

9. Helmut A. Hatzfeld, *Literature Through Art: A New Approach to French Literature* (New York: Oxford University Press, 1952), pp. 156–58.

10. See also the regional novels of George Sand (*La Petite Fadette* and *François le Champi*) for a similar portrayal of character.

11. Consult Henri Guillemin's edition of this fragment of *Les Visions* published by Belles Lettres, Paris, 1936.

3—Alfred de Vigny, Preacher in an Ivory Tower

1. See the critical edition of Vigny's posthumous collection by V. L. Saulnier, *Les Destinées d'Alfred de Vigny* (Geneva: Droz, 1947). For rewarding studies on the life and work of the poet, consult P.-G. Castex, *Alfred de Vigny* (Paris: Hatier, 1957). Castex has also published an

excellent appraisal of *Les Destinées* in the series of the "Société d'enseignement supérieure" which appeared in Paris in 1964.

2. *Oeuvres complètes* I (Paris: Louis Conard, 1914), p. 338.

3. The novel, *Stello*, in 1832 and the drama, *Chatterton* in 1835, are accounts of the misunderstood genius of such poets as Chénier, Gilbert, and Chatterton.

4. D. Gallois and J.-B. Piéri, *Le Dix-Neuvième Siècle* p. 125.

5. See Helmut A. Hatzfeld, *Literature Through Art* pp. 160–64 for a discussion of the Romanticist religiosity.

6. The exact ordering of the eleven poems that comprise *Les Destinées* has never been satisfactorily ascertained. The most reliable source on Vigny's intention in the matter is to be found in his own diary, *Journal d'un poète*. The closing section of "Le Mont des Oliviers," entitled, "Le Silence," was added in 1862.

7. Hatzfeld, *Literature Through Art*, p. 160.

8. P.-G. Castex, *Les Destinées d'Alfred de Vigny*, pp. 145–46.

9. *Ibid.*, p. 149.

10. P. Flottes, *La Pensée politique et sociale d'Alfred de Vigny* (Paris: Librairie des Belles Lettres, 1927), pp. 264–65.

11. Contrary to popular belief, "La Mort du loup" was written in October of 1838 and not in 1843. See Castex, p. 75.

12. For a discussion of Vigny and the Positivism of Auguste Comte, see P. Flottes, *op. cit.*, chapter 10.

13. Castex, *Les Destinées d'Alfred de Vigny*, pp. 226–30.

14. Pierre Moreau, *Les Destinées d'Alfred de Vigny* (Paris: Sfelt, 1947), pp. 151–52.

15. *Journal d'un poète* in *Oeuvres Complètes* II (Paris: Gallimard, 1948), pp. 1355–56.

16. Frank P. Bowman, "The Poetic Practice of Vigny's *Poèmes Philosophiques*," *Modern Language Review* LX (July 1965), 363.

4—Victor Hugo and the Prophetic Vision

1. For a popularization of the poet's life, see André Maurois, *Olympio ou la vie de Victor Hugo* (Paris:

Hachette, 1954). Maurois' book is also available in English as *Olympio or the Life of Victor Hugo* (New York: Harper, 1955).

2. See Théophile Gautier's *Préface d'Albertus* (1832) for an exposition of the doctrine of art for art's sake.

3. César Auguste Franck's Symphonic poem of 1884 is inspired by "Les Djinns."

4. Eugène Hugo had gone mad at the time of Victor Hugo's marriage to Adèle Foucher in 1822.

5. Etienne Privet de Senancour, *Obermann* (Paris: Charpentier, n.d.), p. 85.

6. Maurice Z. Shroder, *Icarus: The Image of the Artist in French Romanticism* (Cambridge, Mass.: Harvard, 1961), pp. 84–85.

7. Shroder relates the use of the word *mage* to the light symbolism so prevalent in Hugo's later poetry.

8. Gwendolyn Bays, *The Orphic Vision: Seer Poets from Novalis to Rimbaud* (Lincoln: University of Nebraska, 1964), pp. 111–12: describes the group of writers interested in the occultism of Eliphas Lévi (1810–75), and mentions the presence of such figures as Pierre Leroux, Alexander Weill, Victor Considérant, Emile Littré, and Louis Ménard at séances held at the home of Saint-Simonian, Charles Fauvéty in the 1840's.

9. *Les Châtiments* were published in Brussels in November of 1853 under the title, *Napoléon le Petit*. The definitive title of *Les Châtiments* appeared in the Paris edition of 1870.

10. There are two relatively recent editions of *Les Contemplations*: the first by André Dumas published by Garnier in 1962, and the second appeared in two volumes under the editorship of Jacques Seebacher which was published by Armand Colin in 1964.

11. Gwendolyn Bays, *The Orphic Vision*, pp. 112–14. See also Auguste Viatte, *Les Sources occultes du Romantisme*, 2 vols. (Paris: Champion, 1965).

12. Gustave Simon, *Les Tables tournantes de Jersey, Procès verbaux* (Paris: Conard, 1923), pp. 30–34.

13. Critic Joseph Vianey makes a strong case in his introduction to the *Edition critique des Contemplations de Victor Hugo* (Paris: Hachette, 1922), for support of the view that the various dates signed by the poet are more than unlikely. Vianey proves that ninety-two of the

one hundred and eleven poems, allegedly written after the death of Léopoldine, were composed between 1854-55.

14. Although Hugo claims to have written the poem in January of 1834, references to those works composed only after 1834, in his own career, place the actual completion of the poem in 1854.

15. Pierre Moreau, *Les Contemplations ou le temps retrouvé* (Paris: Archives des lettres modernes, 1962), p. 52.

16. André Dumas (ed.), *Les Contemplations* (Paris: Garnier, 1962), p. 436. Dumas argues that the poem, "Ce que dit la Bouche d'ombre," is directly related to the séances that took place on 22 October 1854, and may be attached to the "metaphysical" cycle which includes "Ce que c'est que la mort," completed on 1 November 1854. The poem, "A Celle qui est restée en France," ends *Les Contemplations* on a more personal basis.

17. H. J. Hunt, *La Légende des siècles de Victor Hugo* (Oxford: Blackwell, 1957), pp. vii-viii. For the complete critical edition of the epic, see P. Berret, *La Légende des siècles*, 6 vols. (Paris: Hachette, 1921-27).

18. Hunt, *ibid.*, p. 223.

19. *Ibid.*, p. 224.

5—Musset and the Poetry of Experience

1. P. Gastinel argues convincingly that the major poetic production of Musset does not so completely hinge upon the emotional crisis of 1833-34. Gastinel proves that Musset returned to his earlier poetical themes after 1834. See P. Gastinel, *Le Romantisme d'Alfred de Musset* (Paris: Hachette, 1933).

2. Geoffrey Brereton, *An Introduction to the French Poets: Villon to the Present Day* (London: Methuen, 1960), p. 141.

3. René Canat, *Du Sentiment de la solitude morale chez les Romantiques et les Parnassiens* (Geneva: Slatkine Reprints, 1967), p. 10: "He has the good fortune of being half consoled by the belief that memory is sweeter than passion and that happiness consists not so much in loving as having loved."

4. Canat, *ibid.*, p. 12.

5. The pelican image is derived from the medieval bestiaries, and represents a type of Christ.

6. The theme of the double enjoyed a certain vogue during Musset's lifetime. The technique was utilized to good effect in the poetry of Heinrich Heine (1797–1856), notably in his *Der Doppelgänger*.

7. Philippe van Tieghem, *Musset* (Paris: Hatier, 1944), p. 116.

8. Georges Poulet, *The Interior Distance* (Ann Arbor: University of Michigan, 1964), p. 184.

9. Jean Nicolas Arthur Rimbaud, "Lettre à Paul Demeny," 15 May 1871.

10. In 1838, Musset met the celebrated actress, Rachel. He became very interested in her as well as in the revival of Classical tragedy in France.

Bibliography

ANTHOLOGIES

Galland, Joseph and Cros, Roger. *Nineteenth-Century French Verse*. New York: Appleton-Century-Crofts, 1959.

Grant, Elliott M. *French Poetry of the Nineteenth-Century*. Second Edition. New York: MacMillan, 1962.

Parmée, Douglas. *Twelve French Poets*. New York: David McKay, 1962.

Shroder, Maurice Z. *Poètes français du dix-neuvième siècle*. Cambridge, Mass.: Integral Editions (Schoenoff), 1964.

GENERAL STUDIES ON ROMANTICISM

Bays, Gwendolyn. *The Orphic Vision: Seer Poets from Novalis to Rimbaud*. Lincoln: University of Nebraska, 1964.

Brereton, Geoffrey. *An Introduction to the French Poets*. New York: Barnes and Noble, 1960.

Canat, René. *Du Sentiment de la solitude morale chez les Romantiques et les Parnassiens*. Geneva: Slatkine Reprints, 1967.

Gallois, Daniel and Piéri, J.-B. *Le Dix-Neuvième Siècle*. Paris: Eugène Belin, 1960.

Gilman, Margaret. *The Idea of Poetry in France from Houdar de la Motte to Baudelaire*. Cambridge, Mass.: Harvard, 1958.

Hatzfeld, Helmut A. *Literature Through Art: A New Approach to French Literature*. New York: Oxford University Press, 1952.

Hunt, H. J. *The Epic in Nineteenth-Century France*. Oxford: Blackwell, 1941.

Hunt, H. J. *The Epic in Nineteenth-Century France.* Oxford: Blackwell, 1941.

Levaillant, Maurice. *Le Romantisme* in *Neuf Siècles de Littérature française.* Paris: Delagrave, 1958.

Michaud, Guy and Tieghem, Philippe van. *Le Romantisme.* Paris: Hachette, 1952.

Moreau, Pierre. *Le Romantisme.* Paris: Del Duca, 1957.

Moreau, Pierre. *Ames et thèmes romantiques.* Paris: Corti, 1965.

Praz, Mario. *The Romantic Agony.* New York: Oxford University Press, 1951.

Salomon, Pierre. *Précis d'Histoire de la Littérature française.* New York: St. Martin's Press, 1964.

Shroder, Maurice Z. *Icarus: The Image of the Artist in French Romanticism.* Cambridge, Mass.: Harvard, 1961.

Viatte, Auguste. *Les Sources occultes du Romantisme.* 2 volumes. Paris: Champion, 1965.

ON LAMARTINE

Cognets, Jean des. *La Vie intérieure de Lamartine.* Paris: Mercure de France, 1913.

Guillemin, Henri. *Lamartine, l'homme et l'oeuvre.* Paris: Boivin, 1940.

Lucas-Dubreton, J. *Lamartine.* Paris: Flammarion, 1951.

ON VIGNY

Bowman, Frank Paul. "The Poetic Practices of Vigny's *Poèmes Philosophiques.*" *Modern Language Review* LX (July 1965), 359–68.

Castex, P.-G. *Alfred de Vigny.* Paris: Hatier, 1957.

Castex, P.-G. *Les Destinées d'Alfred de Vigny.* Paris: Société d'enseignement supérieure, 1964.

Flottes, P. *La Pensée politique et sociale d'Alfred de Vigny.* Paris: Belles-Lettres, 1927.

Guillemin, Henri. *M. de Vigny; homme d'ordre et poète.* Paris: Gallimard, 1965.

Moreau, Pierre. *Les Destinées d'Alfred de Vigny.* Paris: Sfelt, 1947.

Saulnier, V. L. (ed.). *Les Destinées d'Alfred de Vigny.* Geneva: Droz, 1947.

ON HUGO

Barrère, J. B. *Victor Hugo, l'homme et l'oeuvre.* Paris: Boivin, 1952.

Dumas, André (ed.). *Les Contemplations.* Paris: Garnier, 1962.

Glauser, Alfred. *Victor Hugo et la poésie pure.* Geneva: Droz, 1957.

Hunt, H. J. (ed.). *La Légende des siècles.* Oxford: Blackwell, 1957.

Levaillant, Maurice. *L'Oeuvre de Victor Hugo.* Paris: Delagrave, 1931.

Levaillant, Maurice. *La Crise mystique de Victor Hugo, 1843–1856.* Paris: Corti, 1954.

Maurois, André. *Olympio ou la vie de Victor Hugo.* Paris: Hachette, 1954; *Olympio Or The Life of Victor Hugo.* New York: Harper, 1955.

Moreau, Pierre. *Les Contemplations ou le Temps retrouvé.* Paris: Archives des lettres modernes, 1962.

Seebacher, Jacques (ed.). *Les Contemplations.* 2 volumes. Paris: Armand Colin, 1964.

Simon, Gustave. *Les Tables tournantes de Jersey, Procès verbaux.* Paris: Conard, 1923.

Vianey, Joseph (ed.). *Les Contemplations.* 3 volumes. Paris: Hachette, 1922.

ON MUSSET

Cassou, Jean. *Les Nuits de Musset.* Paris: Emile-Paul, 1930.

Gastinel, P. *Le Romantisme d'Alfred de Musset.* Paris: Hachette, 1933.

Pommier, Jean. *Alfred de Musset.* Oxford: Clarendon, 1957.

Tieghem, Philippe van. *Musset.* Paris: Hatier, 1944.

Index